Chaco Ch

Life and Translation in Argentina

Robert Lunt

Translator Yolanda proudly holds large copy of Wichi Bible

LOXWOOD PRESS

1

ISBN 978-1-908113-62-7

Published by Loxwood Press
50 Loxwood Avenue, Worthing,
West Sussex BN14 7RA

Printed by CZ Design & Print
Unit 3 Southmill Trading Centre,
Bishop's Stortford CM23 3DY

*Dedicated to my special friends
and fellow workers, now at rest with God*

**Pastor Isidro Vilte
Señora Yolanda Alfaro
Pastor Juan Toribio
Pastor Ponciano Benítez
Señor Francisco Pérez
Señor Antonio Segundo**

and

Bishop Mario Mariño

The language of the spear! Author and Francisco at work

Translators Isidro and Yolanda (r) with his sister Isabel

Contents

PART 1

PART 2

PART 1

1

Pointing the way to Peace

Francisco studied the tip of the spear, smiled an engaging smile, and gave me in his language the word I sought. I noted it down in those pre-digital days on a 5"x3" index card, one of many that would in time form the basis of a dictionary.

We were sitting in the open air at a small village on the banks of the River Pilcomayo in northern Argentina. A woman walked by carrying a large earthen water jar on her back, the belt attached to its handles creasing her forehead. Another passed conveying an impressive bundle of wood suspended in a similar way, fuel for the fire outside her simple home of wood and branches with mud roof. Scrawny dogs and chickens rooted around for something edible.

The village is called Misión La Paz, 'Peace Mission', and was established in 1944 by missionary George Revill. Its name reflects the radical transformation in the lives of the indian peoples of the north of the country, a sea-change largely brought about by Christian teaching. This arrived in the first part of the 20th century thanks to pioneer Anglican missionaries and their immediate successors, and 'Peace Mission' is a place where three formerly warring peoples now live together – the Wichi, the Chorote and the Chulupí.

So, what had brought me to this far-flung spot, on the border between Argentina and Paraguay, to learn the language of Francisco and his Wichi (pronounced Wee-CHEE) people? And where else had my adventure taken me before those encounters?

Letters and leaves

Whether it was the bag of letters of the alphabet that my parents bought me when I was very young, I don't know. But something early sparked my fascination for the written word. I'm reminded of a future librarian colleague of similar bent saying he'd been captivated by the printed word "since Caxton!"

Whether it was my moving those letters around endlessly trying to create long words on the carpet of our 1888 semi-detached home at Winsford in the heart of Cheshire, I don't know. But something set me on the road towards Bible translation into an Argentine language that I wouldn't hear of for many years, and to come to delight in such gems as:

Olhaihowatshanhit'awethä
"We're not feeling sorry for ourselves"

Whether it was a moment of divine inspiration some years later that led my parents to advise me to study Spanish, I don't know. My grammar school gave me just a night to decide, but the alternative was physics, so perhaps anyone who knows me would think the choice was obvious.

I do know that it was divine inspiration that led me to a brain-and-heart encounter with Jesus Christ in the late 1960s at Nottingham University, where the Christian Union had a strong interest in world mission. Put it all together – faith, mission, a degree in Spanish – and you have the makings of a missionary to a Spanish-speaking country, one of the Latin American ones as Franco dictated Spain's affairs at the time.

But a few extra steps were needed before I headed overseas: a professional qualification in librarianship and three years practising it in Manchester; acceptance by the South American Mission Society (SAMS), an Anglican presence on that continent since the mid-nineteenth century; two years' training and preparation at All Nations Christian College in a leafy part of Hertfordshire; and a three-month orientation course at SAMS headquarters in even leafier Tunbridge Wells. And there would be plenty more leaves where I would eventually live and serve.

"Why do you think they accepted YOU?" asked a puzzled friend

8

from university. "Well, I think it was my dynamic personality," I replied with a smile and consummate irony. It *was* a puzzle. My personality isn't exactly full of Latin fizz. It must have been the Spanish, the goodwill of the interviewers and Godly direction towards an Argentine people-group far more Anglo-Saxon than Latin in character. Also, I was receiving excellent biblical teaching at one of the notable evangelical churches, Holy Trinity Platt in Manchester, whose rector, Michael Cole, would later become chairman of SAMS.

So, on 3rd January 1977 I flew from Heathrow on an adventure that would take over my life for the next 25 years. Argentina was the country chosen for me because the Diocese of Northern Argentina had requested someone to learn the language of the Wichi people and then co-ordinate a new translation of the New Testament into it.

Argentina was not the most desirable of locations at the time. It was led by a military junta that had taken over a failing nation in 1976 and embarked on a ruthless and brutal campaign to rid the land of everyone considered to be a political opponent – the infamous 'Dirty War'. A teacher we knew disappeared and a friend had to flee the country on discovering her name was on a death list. I recall being halted at a police checkpoint on the highway one night in my first month there and looked out of the truck window straight down the barrel of a gun until all identity documents were checked and passed.

My first weeks were spent in the city of Salta, capital of the province of the same name, and travelling around parts of the Chaco, the vast plain dominated by scrub forest bordered by the great rivers Bermejo and Pilcomayo and home to the isolated and overlooked indigenous peoples of Argentina. I began to learn the language of the Wichi under the guidance and tutelage of the diocesan bishop, Patrick Harris. He was a great teacher and advocate of the language in an era when some folk felt the way forward was to focus on the national language, Spanish, and disregard the indian tongues as unfit for the modern world and doomed to wither and die. This gloom was shared by some indians, including one of my excellent language teachers, an elderly Wichi man, who once used the word *museo* (museum) of his

9

language's future, shaking his head as he did so. However, today those languages are thriving, due in no small part to Bible translations and accompanying linguistic studies.

The growing Wichi population of around 50,000 have developed a growing pride in their language, and they and the other indigenous peoples of the Chaco in both Argentina and neighbouring Paraguay can point to the intrinsic value of those languages as a measure of their own inherent dignity. Their languages matter – and so do they.

A flicker of hope

After those initial weeks I was sent, with some apprehension, north from Salta one Friday evening in late February towards the village of two names that was to be my home for the next two years: Algarrobal (site of the *algarrobo* trees, a native hardwood) or Misión Chaqueña (Chaco Mission – being the first Anglican mission established in Northern Argentina back in 1914). I didn't arrive there until the early hours of Sunday and felt tired and desolate, having waited all Saturday in the town of Embarcación, 25 miles away, for a means to get there. In those days no local bus ran along the unmade road. But as I looked out from the back window of my room in the house I was to share initially with agriculturalist Arthur Houston – who'd driven out to Embarcación to meet me and take me to my new home – I realised this was "the end of a long journey's beginning", and saw in the distance the light of a fire trying to penetrate the total darkness of a land still without electricity. It gave me a flicker of hope that all would be well …

Bishop Patrick was thoroughly supportive of the huge and essential task I was called eventually to undertake: the new translation of the New Testament into the Wichi language. "If I weren't fully occupied as bishop", he told me, "I'd love to do it myself." So he generously allowed me the three-year span of my first term of service to study the language and the culture in which it was embedded. My base was Misión Chaqueña but I travelled to different parts of the vast area, including two months in the railway town of Ingeniero Juárez where there were Wichi who'd moved from the south and others who'd come from the north, living on separate sides of the town and speaking their own dialects, noticeably different but mutually intelligible.

After two years I found myself with a good knowledge of Wichi but had any number of conundrums about the structure of the language. Just before Christmas 1978 I went north to the banks of the river Pilcomayo for a two month dialect-study sojourn in Misión La Paz. There two things happened which were to have decisive significance for life, project and ministry.

I met Francisco, a man with a bright smile and great patience, deeply gifted in his beloved language of which he was suitably proud. Francisco Pérez, though an agriculturalist, was to solve for me many of my conundrums.

Also, there was the region's doctor, Margaret Scott, from Sheffield, whom I'd encountered in the city of Salta and with whom I'd then travelled over two days by train and truck to Misión La Paz as she accompanied her patients back home from the city's hospitals in time for Christmas. Two of the patients were babies and we had three nappies, which meant regular washing and holding them out of the train window for the midsummer sun to dry! The whole experience gave us a lot of time to get acquainted and led to a wedding on La Paz's village green (it was predominantly brown) at the end of May 1979. Without Francisco's timely insights and Margaret's constant companionship and love over more than 40 years, there would be neither Part 1 nor Part 2 to this memoir.

We lived successively in Misión Chaqueña, Misión La Paz and the city of Tartagal, by which time our children, Alison and Elizabeth, had appeared on the scene and my father had passed away. It was on Alison's second birthday in 1982 that we heard on the BBC World Service that Argentine salvage workers had occupied the British island of South Georgia, leading to the Falklands War. This came not long after the commencement of the Bible translation in partnership with the incomparable Isidro Vilte, then a Wichi layman, later a respected pastor and archdeacon. Sadly, both Isidro and Francisco have now passed away.

The war eventually caused us to return to the UK for a stay which would last for more than two years and my mother had the opportunity of seeing her young granddaughters. But in August 1984, having been convinced afresh of our calling at a conference of SAMS at Swanwick in Derbyshire, we returned to Argentina and went to live in yet another location, the town of Ingeniero Juárez (from hereon abbreviated to Juárez) where I'd spent time early in 1978. We were to carry out the remainder of our family ministry there in two blocks of three and three-and-a-half years.

2
A town called Juárez

Juárez is like Marmite. Stuck in the middle of the Chaco and with roads which after rain resembled the savoury spread, it was loved by some missionaries, hated by others. In our day it was linked to the provincial capital, Formosa, in the east by a regular bus service along a relatively well-maintained dirt road, and to the town of Embarcación in the west by an erratic bus service along a badly maintained dirt road – and both ways by a fitful rail service. Juárez appeared to the uninitiated bereft of shops apart from three main stores, until you realised that many front rooms of private houses doubled as shops. The local greengrocers was in someone's living-room, though there was also a travelling greengrocer who visited us regularly. With a growing population, new kiosks seemed to open almost weekly.

The three major stores were all on or close to the main street, the *avenida*, unmade like all the other thoroughfares. Two of the stores were owned by families who had migrated from the Middle East and all sold a variety of goods. You arrived with your list and announced each item to the shop assistant who would get it for you. Later in our time there our preferred store became a self-service supermarket, much to the delight of our favourite assistant who heralded it as an extraordinary innovation. We also frequented the small shops and kiosks for basic items like freshly made bread, cheese, cooked meats and *gaseosa* – fizzy drinks, not very healthy but welcome in the often 30-40 degrees heat.

Main meals in Juárez were usually based around a choice of beef or beef: we were, after all, in Argentina. We were blessed by having a home-help whose sister was a butcher; Catalina would let us know when her sister was killing a cow so that we could put in our order. The quality was not that of other parts of the country – the cattle fed mainly on scrub – but was tasty and usually chewable.

Along the *avenida* stands the hospital whose staff during our time included at least six indian auxiliary nurses serving under a doctor from the national capital, Buenos Aires. Under its auspices our long-serving German-born colleague Helen Sohns trained indian village midwives, preserving their traditional ways while enhancing them with modern science. Tucked away in a small dispensary in the Wichi neighbourhood of Barrio Obrero, our Yorkshire colleague Beryl Gilbert worked with an indian nurse diagnosing and treating patients suffering from tuberculosis, one of the scourges of the Chaco. In that same neighbourhood in 1986 new offices were opened to form the administrative centre for the indian churches across the huge Chaco area, an appropriate step forward because of Juárez's central location and its being the long-time home of Assistant Bishop Mario Mariño (of whom much more later).

Juárez might stand in the middle of the Chaco, but our home was definitely not in the middle of Juárez! Years earlier the diocese had acquired land at the eastern end of the town and three single-storey houses were built on the site. In our first term of service there we occupied the largest, originally built as a dwelling for *señoritas* – single-lady missionaries – so had three bedrooms, each opening on to a long living area described with some accuracy by one visitor as "barn-like".

For our second term we moved to the one next door, a long bungalow of three bedrooms, plus a guestroom on the end. Set in a corner of the mission compound, it was built of whitewashed mud-brick with zinc roof panels, false ceiling of polystyrene because of the heat, and floors of either earth or tiles. This was my favourite of the many houses I lived in during my years in Argentina. Inside toilets were installed in each house to replace – or rather supplement – the long-drops which served when I first visited in the 1970s. There was also a building which included a garage for vehicles – all pick-ups, as were most vehicles of the area, sturdiness being necessary to cope with the ruts and bumps of the roads of the town and area. Rooms on either end served as deposits or accommodation at different times. During our final term we had a caretaker, the excellent Emilio Rivero of the

Toba people, who lived there with his family and was an excellent support and jack-of-all-trades.

I don't know if anybody ever gets used to Marmite, but I was one of those rare folk who developed a taste for Juárez. I had disliked it originally but came to see it as home. When we were back living in the UK in the 1990s and I spent up to three months of each year visiting Argentina to oversee the translation of the Old Testament (the New having been completed in 1991), I always felt that to arrive in Juárez was like coming home. It had also been the first place where my wife and I and the family had lived for more than eleven months in our abnormally peripatetic marriage and family life. I recall saying to an Argentine colleague, *"Se puede vivir Juárez o sobrevivirlo"* (You can either live Juárez or survive it). *"Exactamente"*, he replied and hastily drove off!

We all certainly lived it, and it was a life of adventure, friendships and challenges aplenty. Living there was described by one Argentine visitor as *"muy precario"*; yet for the people whose lifelong home was the Chaco, life was much more precarious...

A town called ... Juárez

15

Donkey power in Juárez

The now paved road to the Mission

Our living-room, with translator Juan and cat

Children and church at Misión Chaqueña

17

Preparing the cactus fibre …

…. To make a yica (string-bag)

José Cicka and son drilling a well

3
César

I still remember the morning César turned up at the mission compound in Juárez. We were living in the largest house, another being occupied by the de la Cruz missionary family from Buenos Aires and the third by Helen Sohns. She and ourselves were Wichi-speakers and César came to us as he needed someone who understood his language. He had travelled from his village by the River Pilcomayo with his daughter Arminda who was suffering from tuberculosis. There was no public transport in that area, so you had to beg lifts on any vehicle. They'd travelled in a jeep whose driver was drunk and who struggled to manoeuvre the vehicle along mud-bound roads, as well as almost slipping into a hole when crossing a rickety wooden bridge. They had picked up a lift in an ambulance, but this ran out of petrol and they had had to stop at a ranch. A sick pregnant woman travelling with them died with her unborn child at the ranch. Life was indeed precarious.

César left Arminda at the hospital in Juárez and came to us for a *changa* – a job to earn some money. A path needed to be cleared from the centre of the compound to the rubbish pit in the corner (no refuse collection in those days) and César was pleased at the chance to earn his immediate living, having arrived, as folk often did, with nothing.

He worked hard and his time in Juárez was hard too. A baby *yarará* – a poisonous snake – attacked from a woodpile, but his boot saved him; he was seized in the street by police as an 'unknown' and marched to the station for investigation; and he received news from home that another daughter, aged ten, had died from chickenpox; and finally, Arminda died. I led a hastily arranged funeral service at the Juárez cemetery, a local pastor made a cross for the grave, my translator colleague Isidro carved her name on it, and César erected it. He spent much time with us over those weeks, eating, bathing and sleeping as he battled stolidly but feelingly through his tragedies, the God on whom his faith stood bearing him up. It was a privilege to be with him, serve him, pray with him and learn from him, being reminded that this earthly life, so hard and precarious for so many, was not the only one. "God has still not called me home", other Wichi sometimes said to us, with a mixture of contentment and longing.

No end to precariousness

Next year César arrived by tractor with folk from his community and others nearby to seek support for their Christmas festivities, and he told us that his young son had somehow fallen from his mother's sling at the river and drowned. He said the villager who made the coffin had charged him a shirt, the gravedigger a pair of trousers and the bearer wanted money. I gave César a shirt and Margaret went to buy biscuits and *pan dulce* – the local version of Christmas cake – for his and the other communities.

Three years later César arrived with another sick daughter, Dionisia, in need of blood transfusions. Margaret drove round Juárez seeking donors; I was one who offered my services at the hospital and my half-litre helped save her life but nearly ended mine; it was the hottest day for many months, temperatures surpassing 40°, and I apparently turned deathly white and pulseless. There was no water in the hospital, but I recovered thanks to sugared water produced from somewhere and Margaret's dash across the road to a kiosk for a very large bottle of Coca-Cola. Meantime, someone from the kiosk went to school and told Alison, who was rehearsing for a play: *"Ha fallecido tu papá"* (Your dad has died). Fake news, thankfully.   The tablets Dionisia required were not available at the hospital, but nurse Beryl had received some in error and was able to supply them. Some time later, however, Dionisia passed away, as did another of César's daughters back home. Truly, in a world where life was always precarious, theirs was a family tragedy of huge proportions.

Yet I never heard him – nor anyone else there – ask why God allowed it, why bad things happened to godly people. Once back in the UK my young daughter asked me why English people are sometimes so unpleasant and demanding (not the exact words she used). I said it was because here we're used to *having* – unlike the Wichi – and feel entitled. We as Brits did sometimes wonder about God's providence – but then we'd hear of César, a man who'd lost so many of his children, teaching other people's children about God in his village Sunday School. Faith is believing in a God who is *Lhawuk, Lhaka Niyat*, our Master, our Owner, our Great Chief. He knows best, and while life on earth is temporary, his loving presence is eternal, as 'ever-green' (to translate their expression literally) as the life of whoever believes in him.

4
Missions of mercy

On at least two occasions during our years in Juárez the unstable river Pilcomayo to the north flooded and caused folk to move further inland and resettle, rebuilding homes and church – sometimes not in that order – on higher ground, sadly further from their fish lifeline. In the township of Potrillo one year, only the school (damaged), hospital and carpentry remained. Another village found itself on an island in the river.

Emergency aid would be flown in by the provincial government, which gradually became aware of its responsibility towards these previously forgotten and marginalised people. Awareness and concern often increased in proportion to the need for their votes in whatever elections were on the horizon!

But the missionaries were always near at hand and remained, in bad times and good, the first port of call for help great and small. My diary records that on one day alone Margaret and I had requests for "sweets, money, paint, spectacles, second-hand clothing, English lessons, paper, gas-ring and materials for building a patio." On another, from just one person, a gentle and godly pastor, "blanket, bicycle, second-hand clothing, rope-soled sandals, hymnbooks, a small amount of money". The pastors were not paid, but carried out their ministry voluntarily and sacrificially, as is still the case.

Blackboards and improbable photos
Some things we supplied, some we couldn't, and some we could but didn't where it was inappropriate to cultivate such dependency. I recall a conversation sparked off by a concerned Argentine colleague: "Are we creating dependency by supplying blackboards etc?"

"But this is what they ask for."

"But that's because the *criollos* [the majority race] have them. So, is dignity for the indians to copy the 'dignity' of the *criollos*? Or can they be persuaded they can have dignity without such things?"

Margaret helped the many Wichi Sunday Schools across the Chaco with weekly lesson material and training courses and she was often bombarded with requests for resources. She received one letter which said, in back-translation from Wichi: "We who live in Campo del Hacha are thinking about the Sunday School, you who are a *profesora* we think it would be good if you gave us a guitar, give it to the Sunday School teacher César [the same tragedy-struck man of the previous chapter], and also a blackboard, we haven't got a blackboard, we had a meeting and decided it would be good if you gave a guitar to the Sunday School, you who are a *profesora*, Margarita, and paper with cut-out figures. And that's the end of our message, and may God be with you, you who are *profesores*."

Another request from a Sunday School teacher proved difficult to fulfil: "Please send me photos of Jesus' birth".

Five string-bags = one guitar

Payment for goods was a principle and practice always welcomed, and sometimes it was in kind rather than the money which few had. When guitars became all the rage, Margaret instituted a system of payment by *yicas*. These are the traditional string-bags that the Wichi women make from strong cactus-fibre which they pattern with dyes from the forest. Five *yicas* = one guitar, she calculated, and there was a big take-up with folk arriving from their villages proudly to hand over their products (or their wives' products) and take home their guitars, bought in the city of Salta by our colleagues there and sent to Juárez. They would be welcome instruments for the music groups in the villages to support their church worship.

One day Margaret received a message by short-wave radio, the only real means of communication with other parts of the diocese in those days. The University of Salta wanted 100 *yicas* by a certain date. She sent messages by hand and by radio to reliable folk in river and forest communities. Soon the *yicas* were made and the order supplied, and the university paid in cash.

Nasty

In the past the indian peoples of the Chaco had fought each other with bows, arrows and spears. But the former warriors are now placid, stolid and taciturn, a revolution they attribute to the Christian teaching brought by pioneer missionaries and their successors, all revered by those who knew them. The indians now see themselves as different in demeanour from the *criollos,* the majority race descended from Europeans, predominantly Spanish, Italian and Eastern European. They distinguish themselves in particular from the *criollo* cowboys (known as the *chaqueños*) whose forebears invaded their homeland from the late 19th century onwards with their roaming cattle. "The *chaqueños* are always fighting, but we've been taught God's Word so we're quiet and peaceable", said a Wichi visiting our house from the village of María Cristina. Oddly but typically another proclaimed: "The others follow politics, we follow the old days." "The old days" means the teaching of those early missionaries. The Wichi are a deeply traditional people - *lhakeyis tä pajchehen* (the old ways) are deep-rooted and *misioneros tä pajchehen* (the old missionaries) are venerated!

There were a few Wichi (a very few) who didn't visit us pleasantly. The man who made the coffin for César's drowned son and requested a shirt in payment was notoriously querulous and demanding. One day he went round three missionaries, one of whom was the diocesan bishop's wife visiting from Salta and extracted money for something or other out of each of them. He even aggressively questioned her about the spectacles he'd asked her to get him. She was mystified, finally concluding that his request must have been made 13 years before when she lived in Juárez. Their memories can be long and selective.

Treat me as poor = be kind

But poverty there was, of a kind it's hard to grasp. Certainly, we wondered how these people, basically hunter-gatherers, fishers and growers of fruit and vegetables in their garden plots, survived at times, particularly in the winter season, the time they call *fwiy'et* (cold weather) or *lop* (from which the word for 'thin' comes). At one church meeting I recall prayers which included phrases such as *"Nayahit'a olhamel olhäk, mat ..."* and *"Niwohit m'ak tä otufw, mat is t'at"*, both expressing hunger, lack of food ... "but it's all right" – the characteristic Wichi blend of realism, fortitude and faith.

The Wichi word for 'plead', 'beg', comes from the root for 'poor' and means 'treat [another] as poor' – and therefore, be kind [to him/her]. It's fundamental to the way Wichi society works in their concern, care and kindness to each other, and the missionary presence has become embedded into this way of life. In Appendix 2 on the Beatitudes in Part 2 there are further observations on this issue.

The cattle belonging to the *criollo* settlers have seriously diminished the indians' hunting-grounds and today large commercial enterprises have taken over and deforested much of the land not legally owned by the indians so they can grow crops such as soya for European and Asian markets. The Anglican Church has worked for many years with the people in some areas to gain them the title deeds, achieving success in some areas, but the battle continues. Over the years the Church established agricultural projects in different places, but it was a relentless struggle against nature and the vast distances for travel. I visited María Cristina with agriculturalist colleague José Cicka, Argentine godfather to our daughter Alison, and saw them rejoicing as a well was dug and sweet water flowed. They had previously had to walk five or six kilometres to get river water. Our former Argentine colleague of Irish descent, Alec Deane, continues similar important work.

5
Reginaldo

Always welcome at our home in Juárez was Martín, a lay leader in one of the Wichi churches in Potrillo, 90 kilometres to the north. He once arrived unexpectedly - in reality, the vast majority of visits by the indians were unexpected as there was no easy way to communicate that they were coming. Accompanying him was a young pastor from the area, both having come for a weekend course. They had nowhere to stay and so we put them up as guests in the usually busy 'Hotel Lunt'. I recall we had enjoyable cross-cultural fellowship but I also remember a cross-cultural calamity: my failed explanation to the young pastor of how to use a flush-toilet and Margaret's subsequent displeasure when bucket, mop and disinfectant had to be produced.

Flush-toilets (known as *inodoros* = 'not smelly') were an innovation in Juárez in our day. We had previously used long-drops, situated at a short distance from the houses, often visited by other creatures, memorably snakes, skunks and cockroaches. When we first arrived in Juárez, I recall mass-murdering around 60 cockroaches in and around our long-drop, using a powerful poison. One night by torchlight in electricity-less Misión La Paz, Margaret and our girls encountered a snake on the path to the long-drop, then moments later the girls ran screaming from the said convenience with the cry of "Skunk!" This long-drop was doubly smelly.

One day Martín turned up in Juárez with his ten-year-old son Reginaldo, together with letters from the doctor in Potrillo about the boy's heart-murmur and the need for him to go to the city of Salta for enhanced medical attention. This was the start of a long painful time for the whole family. Their niece had just committed suicide by eating the deadly forest fruit known in Wichi as *onhay* after her man's parents had taken him away from her. This was a main cause of death among the Wichi, followed by tuberculosis. Drugs for TB were available and our nurse colleague Beryl had a special ministry to TB patients, but the drugs were often unavailable for lack of government funds so the church's social ministry would invariably come to the rescue.

Reginaldo's heart-murmur took him and his father to Salta, then on various trips for specialist treatment in the capital, Buenos Aires, a thousand miles away. After one of these trips, funded usually by the government's social action plan and with pocket-money from the diocese, Martín and Reginaldo arrived back in Juárez and turned up at the Mission needing a journey home to Potrillo. I was due to visit communities in a different direction but decided to switch to Potrillo in order to take them home. Emilio, our caretaker, helped me load a bed and mattress for Reginaldo into our pick-up truck to make his journey more comfortable, and we made the trip safely to their home where they were greeted with relief and contentment by the family.

On the way back to Juárez I combined the trip with a call at two other communities, intending to pick up two men and their families who needed to catch a lift with our colleague Chris Hawksbee that afternoon to Bible School in Misión Chaqueña. But one of them had gone fishing and so we returned with his family but without the student himself! A few unauthorised hitchhikers were thrown off after smuggling their way on board and we reached home in time to get the folk on to their next lift with Chris. Miguel, the student-gone-fishing, arrived next day but had to wait three days for a train to get to Misión Chaqueña.

Trains, like any transport in the Chaco, were not reliable and Martín and Reginaldo had one nightmare journey back from Buenos Aires. Having reached our provincial capital, Formosa, without trouble, they set out from there at 3am one Thursday, but at Pirané the train derailed and all but their coach overturned. The whole day was spent there and on Friday they advanced very slowly. But near Pozo Mortero there was a further derailment with the dining-car and a coach turning over. Eventually they arrived at our house on Sunday morning – at least in time to join us for a much-needed Sunday lunch.

Mercy in the interior of the interior
I recall two challenging callouts. Once I was asked to fetch the

husband of a lady we knew from his ranch five kilometres from Juárez but deep in the forest at a place I'd never heard of called Pozo del Anta. He'd suffered an allergic reaction to a bee sting. A colleague of his jumped aboard to direct me along a narrow, winding, potholed road, and the entrance was through a gate not meant for vehicles. It required much manoeuvring, so coming back they took down part of the fence to make it easier. I delivered him to hospital where he was given an immediate injection for his swollen body.

One evening our home-help Catalina called to say a schoolgirl had been badly injured in a road accident near Faure (to the east) and would I go to Fraga (west) to fetch her mother? The girl had been taken further east to hospital in Las Lomitas. I set off at 8pm with Catalina's son, the girl's brother and another lad. On reaching Fraga in drizzle, we discovered the police had failed to let the mother know and bring her there. So we drove on four kilometres, then another four along a narrow track to the ranch where she lived. We brought her back with her man, arriving shortly before midnight, and she continued her long journey to Las Lomitas next day by public transport.

6
A virtuous and industrious woman

Some people find the wife described in the last chapter of the book of Proverbs too good to be true. I'm not convinced; I think I married her! I probably take her for granted much of the time but reading through my diaries for the years overseas I was almost exhausted by the amount and variety of work Margaret did – and went on to do back in the UK. Small wonder a friend here in South Yorkshire said to me one day, "You have a wonderful wife", and an asylum seeker from Iran reckoned there could be no more than 500 women of her kind and kindness in the world.

A trained doctor, Margaret had started life as a medical missionary and was known as "la doctora" in the wide area she served. Then in our years in Juárez she dedicated herself primarily to coordinating the Wichi Sunday Schools, also leading for a time the *criollo* young people's group, and in later days being a preacher at the *criollo* church. Regarding this last ministry, she'd been feeling frustrated at the lack of opportunities for women to preach, especially when newly arrived men were called straight to the pulpit – or lectern, to be precise. One evening the *criollo* pastor, quite unaware of her frustration, turned up at our house saying he felt God was telling him to call on some women to join the preaching ministry as they were being neglected. So he'd come to ask Margaret, who was surprised by joy. "I feel like hugging you", she said. Thankfully she didn't.

No one in the area seemed concerned about the gender of the preacher. The Wichi women were thrilled when a Canadian woman pastor came to visit and preached at the main Wichi church in Juárez. The men seemed happy and had no objections. At a synod on the subject of ordaining women, a much respected Wichi pastor couldn't see what the fuss was about. "Women were the first to meet the risen Jesus, so why shouldn't women be allowed to preach him?" he said. Nowadays ordained women are an essential part of the diocesan ministry, and AMARÉ, the local and regional expression of the Mothers' Union, is playing an increasingly prominent role in enhancing the contribution of women in many dimensions of ministry across the diocese.

Chauffeur, Builder, Teacher, Homemaker etc

Margaret did much more than the church activities mentioned. One day Martín and son Reginaldo, noted above, needed to embark on a medical trip to do with the lad's heart problem. Margaret rose at 5:30am and travelled with Assistant Bishop Mario's driver to their home in Potrillo to pick them up, also battling through sandy stretches to another community nearby to buy *yicas* for the University of Salta. They arrived back at our house very dirty but with fish they had bought there. She gave Martín, Reginaldo and a woman traveller a meal and the woman enjoyed a bathe in our girls' paddling-pool.

That night, while I was at a very long church meeting, Margaret drove Martín and son to the bus-station for the overnight bus to Salta, which didn't arrive until after midnight because of a gearbox problem. It had been a murderously hot day and we finally collapsed into bed at 1:30am after a 20-hour day.

On another day I recorded her as driving Alison and Elizabeth to school for their 8am start, and also take an Israeli doctor who was living with us to hospital for work. Then she had to drive to the bus-station to meet a children's church worker who had come on a long-distance bus from Salta to lead a course for Sunday School teachers. Next she drove to a Toba village an hour or so away to bring in some teachers for the course, which began in late afternoon at the local Pentecostal church. In addition, she took an old machine from the mission garage to a man who wanted to clean his typewriter, drove Alison to gymnastics practice, and picked up her Sunday School assistant coordinator, Juan Toribio, to take to the course.

She was also Margaret the Builder, as she devoted herself to acquiring materials for various essential projects. One day she borrowed a colleague's truck to fetch cement, whitewash and iron for

31

work to be done on the colleague's bathroom. Another time she was dashing around day after day buying materials for work on another bathroom because the builders never seemed to know how much was needed. For one project we went to the local reservoir to pick up 250 bricks made by the Pentecostal pastor, Eliseo. Unfortunately, we had confused two brick makers of the same name and the Eliseo we encountered was a lad who seemed to have little idea of the price and less of mathematics; but we sorted it all out. I note that later that day, after loading and unloading the bricks, we took our caretaker to chop wood for his family and had a picnic together. Then it was back to church at night for Alison and myself; I preached while Margaret enjoyed a rest, but we were both exhausted when we got to bed.

All this time she was home schooling the girls in English and maths, making costumes for them for state school activities, visiting sick folk in hospital and their homes, cooking for unexpected visitors at unexpected mealtimes, testing folk's eyesight and supplying second-hand glasses sent from the UK, and amassing those *yicas* made by Wichi women, firstly in exchange for guitars for their husbands and sons and later to supply to the university. Our friend José Cicka was not impressed with this last ministry – he claimed the people needed fewer guitars and more spades!

7
Two Antonios

Margaret invited an alcoholic lad called Antonio to lunch on his fifteenth birthday. She made him a cake and bought him jeans, but we ate outside because of his reputation as a thief. Another day she gave him a job cleaning up the grounds, only for him to return drunk in the afternoon and incur a stiff rebuke. Then he turned up injured and seeking help because the police had had him in for two or three days on a charge of theft. So Margaret went to visit his parents, his employer and the police chief, who said the lad was a regular thief, but usually returned stolen goods. He denied the police had beaten him and the doctor couldn't be sure how he had got his injuries.

There was a second Antonio who had similar problems, and one day Margaret with a Toba co-driver left at 7am for Las Lomitas, three hours away, to take this Antonio to the child magistrate. The officer committed him to his mother's care with the threat of internment in an institution in the provincial capital, Formosa, if he ran away or committed further crimes. While in Las Lomitas, Margaret took (midweek) Sunday School in two neighbourhoods and on the way back called at the community of Bazán to pick up three Wichi women church leaders whom she'd left there in the morning to run a conference.

Tragically, this second Antonio was soon afterwards found dead in the reservoir in his neighbourhood. Margaret was called to take his body to the cemetery where she helped the Wichi pastor lead the service. This second Antonio was the fifth young person to die an alcohol-related death in a few months.

Education was improving for the Wichi, but jobs were few and far between. The brighter ones were able to train as teaching assistants or nurses and one or two were starting to go to university, a trend that has grown and developed in recent times. But for others life remained a struggle and alcohol was an understandable but transient attempt to provide comfort. Drugs have joined the tempting pitfalls since our time there. Yet the church grows with many young people still involved, particularly in the villages away from the urban centres. Music attracts and many youngsters find purpose in forming themselves into groups and acquiring instruments to accompany traditional and modern songs and hymns in Wichi, Toba and Spanish. They might need spades, as José maintained, but guitars are necessary too!

Teresa

The Toribio family are frighteningly intelligent. Juan, the father, now deceased, was Margaret's helper in the preparation of Sunday School materials and later a key member of the Wichi Old Testament translation team, and his genes and those of his wife Carmen are with their many children and grandchildren. During our time in Juárez their daughter Teresa was gifted enough to attend university in the city of Salta, as was another Wichi girl called Elizabeth. Margaret assisted them with getting certificates from their schools in Juárez to say they had completed certain subjects. She also helped them with travel costs and basic necessities such as blankets, giving Teresa lunch one day (for which she arrived an hour-and-a-half late!) and arranging for reliable folk to take to Salta the certificates still required after the girls had travelled.

There were obstacles such as the Argentine bureaucracy (known with characteristic humour as *burrocracia* from the Spanish *burro,* donkey). On one occasion when Margaret was in Salta she radioed me with instructions to get a certain certificate for Teresa. I first sought the wrong head teacher, then the wrong secretary, then the wrong home, but got there in the end. On another trip to get a certificate for Elizabeth the truck she was driving became locked in a deep rut and three lads had to dig her out. When she reached home she discovered her purse and ID were missing. She reported her losses to the police and arranged for a message to be broadcast into the main Wichi neighbourhood via its loudspeaker. Two days later the missing items reappeared, found by some lads at the spot where the truck had been stuck. The local money was gone, but the £10 sterling note was there; the lads had tried to change it, but the main storekeepers, having been forewarned by one of our colleagues, refused to change it.

Teresa began her university course but didn't complete its gruelling schedule. However, she went on to train as a nurse and her father was proud and delighted.

8

A school to remember and treasure

Margaret's ministry extended to the local primary school where she would eventually find herself on the co-operative as a kind of school governor. Escuela 24 (Provincial School No. 24) was ten minutes' walk down the then dirt road called Calle Salta and was where our daughters began their education, Alison doing kindergarten and pretty much all of her primary there and Elizabeth following on two years later. Most pupils were *criollos*.

It was a school of basic resources, blackboard and chalk being the teachers' technology, and with plentiful interruptions for strikes and festivals. The school year ran officially from March to November, with the hottest months of December to February kept for a long summer break. Even that might not be long enough. After her kindergarten year Alison should have started first grade in March 1986, but despite the long break things were still not ready. This was due to a new school opening on the other side of town, a request by the Wichi that another school should be purely for their children, and a lack of school furniture. The postponement turned out to be shorter than we'd been advised: one midweek morning our neighbours' boys, Juan Francisco and Camilo, dashed in just before 9am to say classes were beginning that day. So it was a sudden and unexpected start to primary school for Alison; however, when she got there, having been prepared in haste and proudly wearing her school *guardapolvo* (school smock or 'dust-guard'), she and the other first graders spent the morning sitting around. Next day she finally began classes at the scheduled time of 8am, walking to school with the boys.

More obstacles to an education

A few weeks later Margaret and Alison arrived at school to find the teachers clustered round a radio trying to discover if they should be on strike. They should, so mum and daughter came home. It wasn't

36

unusual. One day teachers and other staff suddenly went on strike at 10am so the children sat bored for two hours until it was time for midday school-out. This strike was over pay (the usual reason) and lasted a fortnight; teachers were not well paid and so disruption was understandable.

The school years of 1988 and 1991 also began late because of pay disputes, and then further delays ensued for Elizabeth whose teacher each time was stuck in Formosa unable to travel because of road and rail conditions – it was still the rainy season. 1988 was her year in first grade but she and other children were sent home early from their streaming test because of a lack of chairs. Margaret was livid Elizabeth had been sent home alone and went to express her feelings to the head and deputy. Elizabeth had the sense to walk to the home of a lady we knew and her teenage daughter accompanied her home. The head and deputy decided she did not need to do the test and could go straight into the top class (i.e. the morning one) the following Monday. Hmm! Come Monday she was up and dressed at 4am ready for school!

Another time Margaret found Alison and her friend Paulina wandering the streets near our house selling bingo tickets to raise funds for school. Apparently, the whole class had been sent out to do it. Margaret drove them straight back to school and fired more stern words at the headmistress. To be fair, the head was an excellent teacher and administrator who gave her life to the school and community, and the day she retired Alison came home in tears. We attended her moving farewell celebration.

Fundraising for school could take different forms. One time Margaret, helped by the girls, spent much of the day at school preparing ingredients for thousands of empanadas, the delicious savoury Argentine pasties, to be sold at a fundraising event. After I'd been to evening service in the town church I went to school and found what seemed like the whole of Juárez there. A healthy profit was made on bingo, lottery and eats, then it was back home for us to a late supper of – guess what.

Strikes were the main obstacle to a fluent school year, but weather

37

could play a part. Sometimes it rained so sub-tropically – the Tropic of Capricorn crossed the Chaco – that it was impossible to get to school and return clean and dry. One day after a morning storm Elizabeth arrived home soaking and dirty, having fallen into the roadside ditch. The last month of the school year of 1988 had classes starting at 7am because of the excessively hot November days; then the school year concluded suddenly and prematurely to spare pupil and teacher further agony in the 46-48° heat.

What Day is it?

The other main obstacle to the educational flow was the ubiquitous *feriado* – the public holiday. School would stop for a day or two to celebrate one of the following:
– Day of the Flag
– Day of San Martín (liberator of the nation from the Spanish colonisers)
– Day of the Race (celebrating the mainstream Argentine Race and Columbus's so-called 'discovery' of the Americas – not overly popular with the indians this one, as their ancestors had been there long before)
– Day of Tradition (this was very conventional)
– Day of the Frontier Police
– Day of the Child
– Day of the Student
– Day of the Educator
– Day of the Teacher
– First Day of Spring
– Day of the Virgin of Juárez
– Day of the Founding of Formosa
– Malvinas Day (Falkland Islands).

I was hoping for a Day of the Bible Translating Missionary but couldn't put my finger on one so had to keep working!

There was always a day off for these celebrations – and sometimes a day off to recover from the day off – and on one occasion a day off to get over the second day off! If there was an election – there were

38

frequent elections – it would take place on a Sunday and the school was the polling booth. So no classes on Monday to clean and disinfect – and probably on Tuesday so the cleaners and disinfecters could have a day off.

Loving our adopted country

Argentina is a proud and patriotic country and the music of the national anthem always stirs me. It would stop me in my tracks and I would stand, headwear removed, and acknowledge the nation's honour, as is expected of all citizens when the anthem plays. Every morning the raising of the national flag took place at School 24, as at every school across the nation, and I was particularly proud to take some visitors from the UK there one morning to witness the ceremony and to discover the flag-raiser was Alison! It reminded me of the time that she was the only child in her class to know the words of the 'Hymn to the Flag', which prompted the appalled teacher to shame the rest of the pupils with the words, *"¡Y Alison es inglesa!"* Alison and Elizabeth stood out because of their fair hair and complexions, yet both 'lived' Juárez, Argentina and school to the full. They participated in the main national celebrations, sometimes dressed up in the processions as peasants from 1810, the year of liberation, and for the special school events. At the closing ceremony to the 1989 school year Alison performed the tango with a boy called Miguel, which led one friend to exclaim, *"¡Qué aculturación!"* – "What cultural adaptation!"

Wherever they were they would sing the patriotic songs they learned at school, something which gave us great pride; they loved their adopted country and have been back to visit several times. However, when young they were not always discerning about their patriotism. In 1987 we travelled home for UK leave with the Spanish airline, Iberia. Not an appropriate moment, you might think, to hold forth with a song about the great liberator, San Martín, crossing the Andes in the early 19th century to deliver whole South American peoples oppressed by those dastardly Spanish colonialists. But Alison and Elizabeth sang it out loud and clear across the cabin. Fortunately, the Spanish crew saw the funny side of it and I still got my salted peanuts.

Primary School no. 24

Raising the flag before classes

School Procession for National holiday

Caretaker Emilio with two of his grandchildren and our daughters

41

9

School governor

Margaret and Alison went one evening to a meeting of the school cooperative and Margaret was elected on to the committee. At the next meeting the headmistress announced the latest financial crisis: the province was unable to supply funds towards school dinners and the school was in debt to the tune of £400 to the main local store. She said only 100 of the 700 pupils came from families able to support themselves. One family with five children and an apparently acceptable standard of living had come to her asking to have any old clothes she received passed on to them.

Back in the Mission a group of us, with Diocesan Bishop David Leake in attendance on one of his visits, discussed the school meal debt, an issue brought into greater focus as the provincial governor had arrived for a big meeting at school. After prayer, David agreed the diocese would pay off the April debt following a promise sent by radio of assistance from Tearfund, the Christian development agency. The diocese would also consider help in paying the May debt and so enabling the resumption soon of meals. Margaret took the news to a meeting of the co-operative and the offer was met with applause for the Anglican Church. At times like this the Falklands War between our nations a few years earlier now seemed long ago and far away. The province would also send a contribution and meals resumed the next week for poor children – who could also bring their siblings. Margaret collected from the bank part of the £4,000 donation from Tearfund and distributed it to our school and to schools in three indian neighbourhoods, Wichi and Toba. The headmaster of the Toba school was astonished, saying that such a donation would clear his school's debts.

Mission fault-lines

But not everyone was happy and the story revealed one of the fault-lines of cross-cultural mission. The excellent Assistant Bishop Mario Mariño, the first Wichi bishop and the first Amerindian bishop of the Anglican Communion, was highly displeased that the donation did not go through his hands. It looked like another instance of missionaries taking charge and the local Christian leaders being overlooked in decision-making.

In an ideal mission world the donation would have passed through Bishop Mario's hands, but it went through Margaret's not because she was a missionary but because she was a member of the committee of the school cooperative. She paid him a visit and in an atmosphere of calm explanation and mature listening, the situation was clarified, confessions were made and the meeting ended in prayer. Margaret also prayed for a Wichi pastor who was making one of his all too regular visits to us seeking work, food and money. Bishop Mario perhaps took the hint from her prayer, for he was soon sitting down with this pastor and his Bible, counselling him and helping him consider his future and escape from the vicious path of no work, hunger, undernourishment, weakness, begging. The pastors were not paid for their work and had to earn their own income or hunt, fish and live off the produce from their garden plots.

Cultures easily collide or rub uncomfortably against one another. Mario once came to me to complain about a missionary: "Who does he think he is? He's just been to my house bringing his …!"

Can you complete the sentence? Dog? Dinner? Shiny new truck? No! What the man brought that so upset the bishop was his … diary!! He had come to plan some possible future events, but … "We don't live like that. We don't live for the days to come. We live for this day. And we live for the days that came before."

I sympathised both with the missionary and the bishop. Being a westerner who likes to know what's happening next week and next month, I too found the indians' living from day to day difficult to work with at times – yet thoroughly understandable for a people whose livelihood from forest and river arrived in that way. And as for "the days that came before", where the people have come from and what has led up to today is of supreme importance. It forms their identity and forges their culture. Sit down by an indian fire at night and you see how soon someone starts to reminisce about *ifwalas tä pajche*, the days that came before, the days that are past. Nowadays you will frequently find that the missionary contribution and the Gospel they brought is a part of that conversation, that past, that culture, that identity. Thanks to sensitivity and growing understanding, two worlds have rubbed alongside each other to the blessing of both.

Just keep your diary out of sight!

10
The Wonder of this Church

I once travelled with Assistant Bishop Mario back from a visit to certain Wichi communities. It was a moonlit night along the lonely Highway 81. Then we saw the lights of a vehicle in the distance approaching from the opposite direction. When we met, both trucks stopped and all occupants alighted and began conversation. The folk in the other vehicle were *criollos* and clearly knew or knew of the indigenous bishop. Very soon Mario was preaching the Gospel to them, warmly, graciously, gently but resolutely, and they received with gratitude and deep respect his wisdom and grace, bowing their heads as he prayed.

Years had passed since the indians were seen as barely human in the eyes of the *criollos*. When the first Anglican missionaries arrived in Northern Argentina in 1911 after fruitful evangelistic and 'civilising' work among the tribes across the border in Paraguay, they were seen by the indians as a buffer between themselves and the *criollos* – in the form of settlers come from outside the Chaco together with police and other authorities sent there to maintain order. Those pioneer missionaries won the favour and respect of the indians, not least through learning their languages and ministering to them through education, basic healthcare, setting up stores to help with food supply, translating parts of the Bible, and teaching them the good news of a good creator God and his Son who came among us in Jesus. Learning the indigenous languages was a sound 'political' move as well as the best means of communication because Spanish was the language of the other 'invading' settlers.

Crane for a derailed train
Until the arrival of those pioneers the indians had little concept of a benevolent providence, being animists who lived in fear of spirits in forest and river. The Wichi called such spirits *ahät* and an adaptation

of that word – *ahätäy* – came to be their term for the *criollos*, probably because of their behaviour and their hostility to the indians – or because their skin was light, as was that of spirits. This latter and more charitable explanation was proffered to me one day by a Wichi man with many *criollo* friends.

It took a patient eleven years' work before the first baptisms took place in 1922, and from those eight individuals the Wichi Anglican Church was born. It grew and flourished down the years, and eventually in 1966 some of its loyal leaders, gifted in pastoral work and evangelism, were ordained. Mario was one of them and his consecration as bishop followed in 1975, by which time many more indigenous men had been ordained and many more churches had sprung up. In 2011 I visited the Chaco to participate in some of the events celebrating the centenary of the arrival of those first missionaries. A proud year indeed and proud times for a people whose future had looked so unpromising at the turn of the twentieth century. One Wichi pastor compared the coming and work of those pioneers to a crane he'd seen righting a derailed train.

Back in the UK I was seeking some information in the archives of SAMS when my eye alighted upon a minute in the record of the General Council for 1910: "Resolved: to begin a mission to the indians in the north of Argentina". That bare minute spawned more than a century of ministry, resulting in around 160 Anglican congregations spread far and wide across the Chaco. Most are led by ordained folk, both men and women, and there is also a strong lay ministry. Thanks to missionaries, but particularly to the indians themselves – and most of all to Almighty God – it can be said with Bishop David Leake, who was born in the Chaco and went on to lead both Anglican dioceses in Argentina, that "the work initiated in 1911 ... is one of the outstanding stories in Christian mission" *(Under an algarrobo tree, p.147-8)*.

Ancient or Modern

Worship among the indian churches is based on the Anglican pattern: parts of the 1662 Prayer Book were translated into their languages by the early missionaries, and while this may seem a cultural aberration, it provided a form into which the indians could comfortably place their worship and which was appropriate to their traditional ways and patterns. In Wichi this has been updated and modified over the years with their own input, starting with a committee which I hosted in the late 1980s and early 1990s, some details of which are found in Part 2. Hymns and choruses in the early days were translated from English hymnals such as *Ancient and Modern* and *Golden Bells* and incorporated into the service book in a volume that slipped easily into a *yica*. Subsequent editions have retained the format while removing lesser-known hymns and choruses and introducing more recent compositions translated from Spanish or English.

The call for more lively, less structured worship has been met by *alabanzas*, praise gatherings bringing a freer, Pentecostal style that has proved more appealing to younger people and to some older ones too. Choruses in Spanish and the indian languages dominate these gatherings which are often held after dark and do not clash with the traditional services. The music is supplied by local groups with guitars, accordions and other instruments, including *bombos* – drums frowned upon in our day by the older indian Christians as having provided the beating backdrop to the pagan ceremonies of their past, ceremonies often fuelled by alcohol and leading to immorality, violence, and sometimes murder.

11
Bishop Mario and his colleagues

Assistant Bishop Mario was a godly man and there have been many others.

Alberto González, ordained with Mario in 1966, was a much loved pastor and evangelist whose memory is celebrated in the downstream churches of the River Pilcomayo, the area where he originated. He also played a major role in the first complete translation into Wichi of the New Testament, published in 1962, and was brother-in-law to Isidro Vilte who was senior translator of the Wichi Bible of 2002. Alberto's marital life was not as happy as it should have been; both his wives, who were sisters, deserted him, the second for a younger man, and Isidro told me how shortly afterwards their daughter came to Alberto with a request from her mother for *mate* – green tea as much loved by the indians as by the *criollos*. Alberto gave her some, and graciously added pasta, sugar and flour, with the wish that she and her new companion "eat well". Though Isidro was brother to both wives, he held his former twice-over brother-in-law Alberto in the highest regard.

For all the saints
Another saintly old pastor also saw his wife go off with another man, but this woman returned to her husband next day, much to his surprise. The community had called on him to go after her and punish her, but he declined, preferring to preach forgiveness. When she returned he welcomed her and gave her a meal. Some Christian teachings were taking firm roots.

Younger pastors who stand out are people like Gulasio and Crisanto. The latter is now an assistant bishop in the diocese and visited the UK in the 2000s. He had been soundly trained by the beloved Pastor Mariano Pérez. Mariano, who lived into his nineties, was converted as a young man and steadfastly faced up to the hostility of witchdoctors in his early Christian years. Unlike the pastors mentioned, he was happily married and I warmly remember him saying to me on my wedding day, *"Nech'e hach'otfwa ihi"* – "Now you have a helper".

Gulasio, who was ordained during our time in Argentina, is strong and steadfast in faith and leadership, a wise man of good sense – *lehusek ihi* in Wichi, 'he has inner being'. My diary records hearing him preach a "clear, concise, direct and advisory" sermon, and manage "to give a word of encouragement from a predominantly admonitory passage" (Galatians 1:1-10), something not always managed or desired by Wichi preachers. At the end of that service he prayed for the needs my wife and I had raised: the Bible translation project, the need for two Argentine colleagues to learn Wichi to enhance their ministry, and the health of an ex-missionary. Many leaders in their prayers tended to stick to familiar issues closer to their community.

Need a roof over our head

Antonio was the lay leader of the church in Barrio Pilcomayo, Juárez; he avoided marital problems by remaining single, highly unusual in the culture. He was faithful for decades in that church and I was saddened when I learned he has recently died. He loved singing the traditional Wichi hymns and had a strong, resonant voice. There was a period when the most important thing in his life was the church roof – there wasn't one – and he prefaced every service with a call for *chapas*, the zinc panels used to cover churches. One Sunday when I was preaching there it was noted that the sun was blazing straight down on me, and so two men were ordered to fetch two old cardboard roof-panels. They clambered up and put them over the hole. It was a kind of reversal of the story of Jesus and the paralytic – putting up a roof instead of removing one in order to facilitate blessing. Later at another service the members gave a generous offering, which was the start of the answer to the need for *chapas*, and was an encouraging example of responsibility being taken by a local congregation.

Buildings and their roofs were often a cause of trouble. One time we were travelling as a family visiting communities near the River Pilcomayo. It was a very cold winter Sunday afternoon and when we arrived in a village we found that roof and brick walls of the church had been removed and taken away after a split in the congregation. When such divisions occurred, one group would sometimes remove parts of the building they considered theirs and move them to another site for reconstruction.

In this village as the sun went down and the bitter south wind from the Antarctic rushed through, we sang the hymn *Y'ahumin Dios lew'et* that I had chosen. Margaret later pointed out to me how totally inappropriate this was on such an afternoon and in such a dilapidated building – we know it in English as "We love the place, O God"!

After fifteen minutes and an exceedingly short message from the visiting preacher – me – we decided we loved the people more than the place, closed the service and the villagers rushed back to their fires and we to our truck.

Cutting words and confecting sins

I enjoyed worshipping and sometimes preaching at Barrio Pilcomayo with Antonio and the small appreciative group. But one day Antonio spent the first five minutes telling everyone that I was there and would preach. The sixth time he said this I managed to interrupt (literally *cut his word* – a grievous sin for the Wichi) and tell him I hadn't known I was preaching and hadn't got a sermon! Thankfully Isidro was there and he *had* got a sermon – Isidro always had a sermon! And mercifully Antonio forgave me for cutting his word.

Isidro and Antonio rarely got things wrong in services, but sometimes a leader would have us scratching our heads or trying to keep a straight face. One layman had an interesting time leading service one morning. Having slipped into a form of Spanish and told us we were now at the time for *Confección de pecados* (Confection of Sins instead of Confession), he then exhorted us to 'confect' and then immediately absolved us before we could confect or confess anything.

Next he reminded us that as Christmas was approaching, we should sing Hymn 47 from the Wichi hymnbook – which happened to be a Palm Sunday hymn. Perhaps he confused Jesus' flight as a baby to Egypt (probably on a donkey) with his triumphal entry to Jerusalem on one, especially as the first line of Hymn 47 says: "The Lord is riding an animal".

12
Special Measures

New churches were always springing up – some with *chapas* (roofs) removed from others! The churches were a sign of God's presence in the heart of a community and also that the people belonged to the Anglican Communion, something of which they are proud. Its global nature means so much to a people who otherwise feel they live in the uttermost part of the earth. Whenever a new church building was ready for use, a celebration would take place to which Bishop Mario and many church leaders from near and far would be invited. We too had the privilege of participating in some of them.

One time I left with Mario and others in his truck for a weekend gathering in María Cristina by the River Pilcomayo, culminating in the inauguration, or dedication, of the new church there on the Sunday. The journey was not easy: a guide we picked up in one community, and who claimed he knew the best way, got us lost and we ended up on a long, lonely road taking us away from the river. We finally arrived at María Cristina in the afternoon and a new brick house was provided for our accommodation. However, the conference organiser had not turned up and the layman-in-charge of the church had gone off to another community to fetch folk. The admirable stalwart Pastor Cefas arrived from his nearby village and so Mario stirred him to get a meeting going. He did and it lasted three hours; I was on as last speaker and in the increasing darkness and with no artificial light I couldn't see to read portions of the Bible passage, having left my torch in the house. I managed to preach and then after a break for a meal lighting was found to illuminate the church for another three-hour meeting!

Enter by the narrow door – once you've cut the ribbon
Next day was the Sunday of the inauguration and at the sound of the bell everyone headed into the mud-brick church to get a place, before Mario realised we hadn't had the ribbon-cutting ceremony. Someone

brought 'ribbon' – a bicycle inner-tube around which a few bits of paper in the national colours of light blue and white were twirled – and everyone was sent back outside. I was then asked to say a word on 'My house shall be called a house of prayer', and after a song and another short message, old Pastor Mariano, provided with scissors, cut the 'ribbon' and in we went, pushing and shoving because the way in was narrow and few were those who would find space to sit.

Confirmations took place during the service, 58 in all, almost half of them young people from María Cristina. This was a definite answer to prayers following the total lack of young people in church when we visited two years earlier. Contrary to the stipulation of the liturgy, the bishop did not preach but handed the job to a pastor from Juárez, who waffled ineffectually for half an hour before concluding what he called a "short" word. Another visiting Wichi pastor whispered wryly to me, "Does he really think that was short?" Holy Communion followed, after a delay while someone went to look for wine.

After many hours the service concluded and we trooped out for a welcome stew and fish freshly caught from the river. We visitors then left and Mario asked me to drive his truck on the first leg home. It felt heavy to manoeuvre and when we stopped at a village I discovered why: 17 people were on the back, some authorised hitchhikers, the rest opportunists who had jumped on unseen.

Lead, unlikely light

Later that same year, Mario invited me to go with him to a weekend conference at Potrillo, and my daughter Alison, who was eight, came along. Conferences were, like church inaugurations, much loved by the Wichi as they afforded folk from different communities opportunity to meet, eat, drink *mate* and share time together as well as worship and receive teaching from the Bible. On this occasion, just as we were setting off from Juárez, Mario suddenly remembered the gearbox needed oil. We called on a local mechanic whose nickname translated as 'Dear' or 'Darling', and noted the battery was dry and so we returned to the Mission for distilled water. We finally left at 6:45pm and after 30 kilometres overtook a tractor carrying other delegates. We stopped to give one of Mario's grandsons a drink and noticed smoke starting to pour from one of the tyres. The brake fluid leaked and so the brake had to be dismantled. Darkness fell.

After an hour we were ready, but then the lights failed. The solution? The tractor came behind so we could make use of its lights, and one of our travelling companions leaned over our truck's cab holding the powerful Worktorch I'd bought during our recent UK leave and projected its beam on the road ahead. Mario was greatly impressed. "Why do we need truck lights when we've got this?" he exclaimed.

But soon we stopped again with the same problem, then another engine fault, and the tractor had to tow us until we reached Potrillo at 1:40am. In the dark we couldn't find the church or the local pastor's house, and so the tractor went in search and had a puncture. Thankfully, the pastor heard the kerfuffle and came to lead some of us to a prepared house, one of the new wooden ones built by the government, but the rest waited in the truck and on the trailer for the puncture to be mended. Alison and I finally lay down at 3:15am on the patio of the house – and I was the first speaker at 9am!

In the afternoon I went to a store to buy new batteries for my torch. The mischievous thought crossed my mind: should I charge them to the bishop's transport account and wait for the incredulous reaction of the sometimes crusty Argentine financial administrator at diocesan head office?!

A great saint: Pastor Mariano Pérez

Pastor (now Bishop) Crisanto visiting UK

13

Otamsek

"Chiwoye lhamel tä fwitses?" a Wichi woman asked one day back in 1981. "What's this about the angry ones?"

"The angry ones? Who do you mean?" She replied with the indians' characteristic imprecise jutting of the chin towards the all-encircling forest, a gesture to be interpreted as '(those over) yonder'.

We remained mystified, musing that the cultural gap was too wide to turn those few words and protruding mandible into meaningful communication – when eureka! It dawned that they referred to the apparently imminent conflict between Argentina and Chile over some islands in the southern seas. Indians like her in the sub-tropical oven of the Chaco, miles from the freezing south seas, miles from Chile, miles from anywhere, had heard over the radio that some people far away were angry and were contemplating war.

Yet these indians were Argentine citizens, with identity documents to prove it, granted to them from the 1960s onwards after pressure on the government, mainly from the Anglican missionaries. When another conflict over austral land erupted in April 1982, some of them received call-up papers, but this time the indians were bewildered about it. The Falkland Islands were light-years from the Chaco, a million degrees colder, and Britain and Argentina were fighting for possession of them. "Yet Britain is where the missionaries have come from, and they brought us God's Good News about Jesus Christ, and we believed in Him. But we also believed they were a holy nation. They had to be to send missionaries all the way from 'the other end of the water' with such News. So why are they now sending soldiers and sailors and airmen? Why have they come to fight us? And why have we got to fight them? *Noj otamsek.*"

Noj? Means "it's over". *Otamsek*? Means our peace, contentment, problem-free time, wellbeing, rest, ease, shalom. Our no-worries, no-fears, no-enemies, no-hunger, no-haste.

Some words defy translation! Yet *otamsek* cuts its way to the heart of Wichi culture. "When I can sit outside my simple house at night and drink my herbal tea; rouse my fire and watch my fish or meat roasting; tell my people's myths and gaze at the Milky Way and the rest of heaven; hear the river-water lap and think of tomorrow's catch; shoo away skeletal dogs and listen to humming-birds; gossip about absent companions and brush away importunate insects; thank Our Master for his world. When I can be as this I have *otamsek*. But on my 20th century novelty, the radio, I hear what 20th century people are doing to each other in a world where it seems that 'everything in the souls is old'. And wait to see if the gendarmes will come tomorrow to call my boys to war .... Where is *otamsek* going to? Surely not into battle against those who brought us God's Words?"

Thus the thoughts of the Wichi. Yet if *otamsek* is eroded by the intrusion of the modern world into Wichi culture with its materialism, diseases and mechanised bows and arrows, it has itself been enriched these many years by the Gospel. As well as pointing their way to personal and corporate salvation, that Gospel has given much needed stability and firmness to the culture. *Otamsek* these days has a deeper meaning. When a missionary originally exiled by the Falklands War returned to tour the forest villages and visit the indians, he was met by a sense of aimlessness, disenchantment, bewilderment – except among the Christians. There he found contentment, peace, wellbeing. Despite British wars and rumours of Chilean wars, despite missionary friends and helpers temporarily or permanently gone, despite angry folk over yonder – *otamsek*, quality *otamsek*, genuine, authentic Gospel *otamsek*, remained. In abundance.

14
The hardest chapter

Back in April 1982 on Palm Sunday morning I preached at one of the indian churches in the city of Tartagal where we then lived. My theme was Jesus, King of Peace – especially appropriate as for two days we had been living against the background of conflict between our nations as Argentine troops had landed on the Falkland Islands, news communicated to us on the Friday by the plumber.

Late that Sunday night after our service with the little *criollo* congregation next door, Australian colleague Stephen Barrett arrived from Embarcación with news that we should prepare to leave first thing next morning. A decision had been taken in the diocese that British missionaries must leave Argentina for the foreseeable future and head for neighbouring Paraguay where our colleagues would receive and somehow accommodate us. Accompanying Stephen were Brits Arthur and Claire Houston who would travel with us, first to Bolivia whose border was not far to the north and from where we should be able to travel to Paraguay. An Argentine colleague from Salta would arrive early next morning to drive us.

It was a doubly painful time. Our daughter Elizabeth, then just three months old, was suffering from a severe intestinal colic that was later found to be caused by parasites. Margaret sat up with her most of that night, also drying nappies in the oven in preparation for our 'escape', while I got to bed at 2:45am. Our colleague arrived at 9:30 and we set off for the border, together with the Houstons and our missionary neighbour Margaret Grebby. Alison's Argentine godfather, José Cicka, accompanied us, distressed by the turn of events. At the border Margaret Grebby was turned back because some authority had failed to stamp her passport on a previous excursion, and so she returned to Tartagal and eventually reached Bolivia by another route. It was the day the British Task Force set out for the Falklands, an overheard topic of conversation amongst the border authorities as the rest of us crossed over in silent melancholy.

In the Bolivian border town of Yacuiba the Houstons and ourselves booked into a hotel, expecting to leave soon for the bigger city of Santa Cruz from where we could fly to Paraguay. But the weather turned against us and floodwaters cut the railway. Road travel also became impossible, perhaps no bad thing as the Bolivian buses of the time were "lorries with seats". On Thursday Arthur discovered there was a plane and we booked and made for the airport. The plane approached and departure beckoned; but then the heavens opened again and because of the dirt surface of the runway the plane was unable to land. We trooped back to the hotel.

We had been introduced to a Hungarian-born naturalised Canadian missionary couple who shared fellowship with us and invited us to their Holy Week services in the Baptist church. They recounted to us the story of the husband's escape from his homeland at the time of the brutal Soviet response to the national uprising in 1956. His account of crossing a field in blood-filled boots from encounters with barbed wire made us feel our own 'escape' was not so dramatic and excruciating.

Return to enemy (?) territory

On Easter Saturday, after days of rain and a phone-call to Bishop David in Salta, we gave up trying to go through Bolivia and took the risk of re-entering Argentina, despite the concerns expressed by the Bolivian border official. We then found the officials on the Argentine side had closed the border – but only to go for lunch! They must have eaten well because we eventually crossed without problem and took a taxi at a very reasonable tariff for the six-hour ride to Salta, passing through checkpoints with no difficulty – the sight of two young children in the back probably helped.

That night we stayed with Bishop David and his wife Rachel, and next morning went to Salta airport for a flight to Santa Cruz. Baby Elizabeth had no passport, only the Argentine identity document I'd managed to get her. After initial hesitation, she was allowed through in Margaret's sling, and we landed in Santa Cruz after a week of getting nowhere! We were accommodated in the American guesthouse of the World Gospel Mission where Margaret Grebby rejoined us after her own lengthy journey.

Safe conduct to Paraguay

Three days later we were finally in Paraguay, though not before further drama at Santa Cruz airport. I placed the documentation on the Immigration desk – two UK passports with Alison inscribed in one of them, and Elizabeth's Argentine ID. The official looked at this and told me: *"No sirve; hay que hablar con el jefe"* ("It's not valid; you'll have to speak to the boss"). But Margaret had already gone through with Elizabeth in her sling; Elizabeth was tiny and thin from parasites and was hardly visible. I was taken to the boss's office and informed: "Señor, it is out of order for an Argentine ID to be used for a journey from Bolivia to Paraguay". But he granted me a certificate of 'safe conduct' (or was it 'good conduct'!) for her and told me not to do it again.

In a propeller-driven Electra we made the two-hour flight to Paraguay. We stayed initially in Asunción with Peter and Frances Tyson and their family of four. Among those joining us in the capital were Dick and Jen Hines; they had only recently returned to Misión La Paz from UK leave and had had to get out of Argentina by being rowed across the River Pilcomayo to the Paraguayan navy station. We tried to make the most of our exile but it was far from easy, not least for Alison whose toys and books had remained in Argentina. However, she and Elizabeth enjoyed their first train ride as a wood-burning engine took us to the town of Areguá; to return we sat opposite the driver on a bus with wooden floorboards and a conductor who would whistle to signal him to proceed. Later, though, we moved into the countryside to Colonia Independencia where the hotel was run by folk of German descent. It was there, following a visit by Maurice Sinclair, then SAMS Personnel Secretary and much later to be our bishop in Northern Argentina, that the decision was taken that we return to the UK for early leave. The sense of disorientation caused by the war, alongside the responsibility of a young family with Elizabeth beginning to put on weight but still very unwell, made the decision a sensible one, hard though it was to leave the Wichi Bible translation project for a time – a time that turned out to be 29 months.

"She's obviously your child"

In Asunción we went to the British Consulate to get Elizabeth included on Margaret's passport so that we could fly home – only to be told this had to be done back in Argentina, in the capital, Buenos Aires! However, the official was not one to let bureaucracy stand in the way, especially in wartime, and noting that "with her red hair she's obviously your child" he inscribed her himself. So we flew back to the UK as the war escalated, and Elizabeth's condition was soon diagnosed and treated. We lived in Sheffield, Congleton and Durham, making friends, visiting supporting churches, trying to do work on the translation, and beginning an interest in and concern for persecuted Christians across the world, a burden that remains with us and informs our prayers every day.

We remained unsure of the future until we met our Argentine friend and colleague Helena Oliver at a conference in 1984. Then a Bible verse that had come to Margaret two years earlier, as we flew in that Electra from Bolivia to Paraguay amidst the uncertain and unpromising future of wartime, held out to us its meaning: "Behold, I have set before you an open door that no one can shut" (Revelation 3:8).

That door opened back into Argentina, to new years of fruitful ministry.

15
"Foreigners only"

I mentioned earlier the Wichi word for a non-indigenous Argentine with its probable pejorative sense. The word they coined for us foreign missionaries simply had a geographic sense: *wajchäs,* 'water-tail', the one who has come from the other end of the water. They couldn't have known in the early days just how far that water, that ocean, stretched!

There was, and probably still is, a preference for the Anglo-Saxon missionary rather than the Argentine. The former had faithfully been coming for a century, the Argentines were latecomers, and the oppression of former years from Argentines was not forgotten. It still rankles, rooted in the indigenous mind, although there have been some excellent Argentine missionaries.

The missionary role has changed since the pioneer days; no longer were missionaries sent out as all-purpose men and women, but they went with specific roles and gifts, to meet specific needs, at the specific request of the Diocese of Northern Argentina. Some of the older indian pastors hark back to the old days. I recall one including in his sermon the point that "the early missionaries had a mandate from God; nowadays they come as, for example, agriculturalists, do their work, then go home." In spite of this, he was pleased that they did come and sometimes stay, "because the Argentine missionaries aren't much good!"

Landslide on the Chaco plain
One of the Argentines stood for diocesan bishop when we were there, with a former missionary from the UK as the other candidate. There was episcopal election fever in Juárez, one of the centres, with many mostly indigenous folk coming in to vote. As most Anglican churches were indigenous and the majority of voters therefore indians, they held the whip-hand in the vote and so the result was a foregone conclusion.

A colleague and I went to the main Wichi neighbourhood to oversee the election and I explained to folk gathered in church that the Argentine's voting-paper was pink and the Anglo's yellow. On mention of the latter, someone turned and informed everyone that the yellow one was for the *wajchäs* (the UK missionary), which was followed by an acquiescent murmur round the gathered throng, meaning 'he's the one to vote for'! Then each voter, at his or her name, filed into the private room, Assistant Bishop Mario's office, and placed into their envelope a pink or yellow slip according to choice. To guard against error of identification, a photo of each candidate was placed behind his appropriate colour, but one woman managed to place the photo rather than the slip into her envelope!

The result was the inevitable landslide and it was radioed to headquarters in Salta. The Argentine received votes from fellow-*criollos* across the diocese, but to no avail (though some years later he did become diocesan bishop). It also transpired that some people had confused the UK candidate with another much respected former missionary of the same Christian name. The newly elected bishop later told me he reckoned that had also helped him!

Criollos

The Chaco was home now not just to indians; settlers had come to settle, bringing their cattle and their trades. When we lived in Misión La Paz the mission established generally good relations with those who had set up ranches in the surrounding area and it was often a pleasure to visit these people, share their warm, humble hospitality and where possible share the Gospel. All this work was in Spanish.

Margaret's medical work opened up friendships with families and she began a Sunday School for the children. Old photos reveal a group of youngsters sitting at old desks in an old schoolroom with few resources. Years later we met one of them in Tartagal; now married with a family and a committed Christian, she invited us to her home for a typically generous meal. We had another wonderful surprise in Salta, at one of our many farewell parties in 1991, when we met another member of that Sunday School, now a mother of three and a member of one of the churches there. The seed sown at those old desks had produced good and lasting fruit.

Sausages delay ordination

In towns such as Juárez, the Anglican Church had been established by an extraordinary missionary evangelist, teacher and pastor, Charles Barr Johnston, supported by his wife Lynn. Charles had spent years travelling down Highway 81 and along its parallel railway line, tirelessly visiting folk and preaching in his inimitably direct and totally unself-conscious way.

His work had led to the planting of churches in a number of townships and to the ordination of some local leaders. These were humble, warm-hearted people who lived lives unnoticed by the outside world and by the Anglican Communion, yet transformed by the Gospel and Charles's zealous pastoring. One of them was known as Tuqui, a person firmly supported by his family and very much a man of his environment. On the day of Tuqui's ordination as presbyter (or priest), two bishops, accompanied by a pastor and three missionaries, drove down Highway 81 to his home and church in the small town of Laguna Yema to carry out the ordination. Unfortunately, he hadn't received the message and was in the act of killing a pig to make sausages. Communications were always hazardous and unreliable, but arrangements were hastily made and the ordination went ahead.

Another excellent pastor was Elena, who still faithfully carries out her ministry despite periods of ill health. We always enjoyed the welcome she gave us when we visited and it was a pleasure to participate in services in her little church.

The Centre Church

The Anglican Church in Juárez was pastored by another Mario and by Marcos, and today is led by Narciso, a carpenter who joined the church as a young man during our time there. Two other churches were planted by its members in those days.

The 'Centre Church', as the main one was known, had four evening meetings a week: Prayer Meeting, Bible Study, Holy Communion, and Sunday Worship. It was often hard to tell the difference as they followed a similar pattern.

Worship was quite different to the Prayer Book inheritance of the indians and had a Pentecostal character akin to their *alabanzas*. It had its own structure based around the singing of choruses and the proclamation of *'La Palabra'* – the word, the sermon. I used to think the only thing Anglican about it was the name on the door; nevertheless, worship in this setting, just like in the very different Wichi setting, was a privilege to be grasped, and to see it making an impact on people's living was a delight.

I used to go to the Communion Service which took place on Saturdays and I was invited to preach fortnightly. This was usually well received, but on one occasion I tried to explain to the gathered throng about some Christians in Rome and Corinth in Paul's day thinking themselves superior to others, and I used a number of times the Spanish equivalent of a derisive term 'super-Christians'. Clearly the message wasn't getting across and probably was not particularly relevant. All I can say is the brethren looked super-baffled.

Pastor Marcos had a favourite passage which was the story of Jesus healing and forgiving the sins of the paralytic lowered through the roof; we lost count of the number of sermons we heard him preach on it, but his teaching and applications were good. Pastor Mario was a good and lively preacher and usually incorporated an evangelistic challenge for visitors and any uncommitted or seemingly lapsed folk. But in one more pastorally challenging sermon he asked each of us: "What sort of Christian are you – a butterfly, an eagle, an ostrich, or a wheelbarrow?" I thought we were more likely to be owls as the service that night started late and finished an hour before midnight.

His future rib

Visiting preachers were a mixed bunch. One young man was visiting the area and was invited to bring a greeting to the congregation, as is the custom. When he told us he had come to visit his future rib, it took me a moment or two to realise he had the story of Adam and Eve in mind and it was his biblical way of referring to his fiancée. I was due to preach that night on fasting, but the visitor turned his greeting into a talk lasting 45 minutes. When the pastor called me afterwards, I said I'd keep my sermon back for another time as we can't fast while the bridegroom is with us.

Another visitor was a hellfire preacher who had a habit of sticking an 's' on to his words, so *bondad* 'goodness' became *bondás* and *la tierra* 'the land' suddenly became semi-pluralised – *la tierras*. When in Yorkshire I later encountered a preacher referring to the "elp of the Oly Spirit", I recalled our man in Juárez years ago.

Nevertheless, we enjoyed that church and there were times when our daughters pleaded with us to go even when we were tired and not feeling up to it. They went to Sunday School there, which was usually led by local folk, though sometimes by Margaret. But there were drawbacks, not least the amount of repetitious singing of choruses and the clapping and arm-waving that accompanied them. Alison decided one day she'd had enough of Sunday School "because it hurts my hands". The lyrics of one much repeated chorus were something like "No words can express how I feel about you, Lord". No words could explain to me why, therefore, the writer bothered to put pen to paper.

Bishop Mario and wife Rosa

Bishop Pat Harris (r) with Bishop Maurice Sinclair, Rev John Sutton (l) and the author

16
All welcome

You wouldn't think that living in such remote places we'd get many visitors.

Wrong! There were times when the meal table was not big enough and when there were not enough beds. One time in the very remote village of Misión La Paz with its limited resources, we and our colleagues hosted eleven visitors – some fellow-missionaries and visitors from overseas come to see what this Anglican work was all about. It didn't help that the missionaries forgot to bring bread with them; there was none in the village at the time, and so for a few days Margaret and Alicia Cicka had to bake for everyone.

Juárez was a little less isolated, but because of its situation in the middle of the Chaco it became the centre of the indigenous work, and so the visitors still poured in. Alison and Elizabeth sometimes had to share a bed and Margaret and colleagues once cooked for 21 people – a record, I think.

On another occasion visitors with different objectives converged. One very early morning – 3am in fact – the daughter of the British Ambassador in Spain arrived on a long-delayed train, then two German anthropologists interested in the indigenous people turned up and stayed with us until an empty house could be made habitable. Next Bishop David arrived with his family, a young friend and a lady come to research a book about the Anglican work. We somehow made room for everyone, though the young man had to camp in our living-room. The researcher was Katherine Makower; her book, *Don't cry for me*, was later published and gives a good insight into the growth of the work since 1911 to the late 1980s. The friendly Germans visited us in England at the end of our next UK leave to wish us well as we prepared to return to Argentina.

All the world's roads lead to Juárez

Many of our visitors were international. One French girl, an anthropology student, burst into tears with culture shock on arrival, but another French girl settled well into a two-month stint at the local hospital as part of her medical training. A further anthropology student, a young Dutchman, suddenly appeared at our gate looking for a means to get to the communities along the River Pilcomayo. We arranged a lift for him with a schoolteacher and loaned him a hammock and mosquito-net. He got there safely and called on us on his return some time later.

The Diocese of Northern Argentina has a healthy companion link with the Diocese of Carlisle. In earlier days there were different links, including the Canadian dioceses of Niagara and New Westminster. Representatives of these visited Juárez, sometimes in groups of four, and enriched our lives, reminding us there was a big wide world out there. I arrived back one day from a Bible translation workshop in another province to find a missionary visitor just leaving and two others arriving in company with four people from New Westminster. Lunch took place in mid-afternoon after beds had been rearranged, Alison moving once more to be with Elizabeth. On another occasion a representative from Canada arrived alone – but this retired Cree Indian church minister caught the imagination of the Wichi and Tobas as he spoke of his own indigenous people's experience amid the surrounding majority culture.

Two Swedish Lutheran deaconesses doing a nine-week tour of the diocese, one of whom was allergic to cats, somehow survived staying with us and our moggy. They found the rather untraditional worship of the 'Centre Church' not really to their expectations or taste: it was 'very Pentecoastal' [*sic*].

A matter of interpretation

There were representatives of SAMS at least once a year. One generously brought Marmite to those of us with a taste for it, spooning it out of a large container she somehow carried round South America.

All such visitors were welcomed in the churches and asked to preach; they also led refreshing Bible studies for the missionaries and brought friendship, diversion and the Word of God into our lives and those of the local people.

Some spoke Spanish, others not, and so interpretation had to be provided for these – as it always did for the Wichi. One visitor taxed my translational skills with references to 'the Father-heart of God' and another to his former life in upholstery. One time Bishop David asked me to interpret from English to Wichi for a visitor from South Africa. During his talk this man mentioned the number 'seven', at which I apparently backed up my translation by raising five fingers. Afterwards David congratulated me on my Wichi but recommended I take a course in mathematics.

The 'Father-heart of God' visitor, John, was a charismatic and was invited after Sunday service to minister to a man who may have been demon- possessed. A missionary colleague and several church leaders joined in, but rather than follow John's instruction to wait in silence for the Holy Spirit to come down, the leaders launched into *Sali*'s (Go, get out!) at the demons. This happened twice, to John's exasperation. After ministry from John, the demon seemingly departed. The man's father was a long-serving lay leader in a church and the man's brother went on to become a very good pastor. He is the person responsible for the translation into Wichi of the chorus *Yesterday, today, forever* – he received the translation in a dream one night and came next morning to share this extraordinary story, and the translation, with me.

More internationals – and an English anthropologist
There were the unlikely visitors, such as the three Dutch tourists who turned up one day. Juárez – tourist spot?! After feeding them, Margaret drove them with Alison and Elizabeth to visit two communities, one Toba, one Wichi. One early morning our colleague Beryl arrived back by bus from Salta accompanied by a young man from Kansas who was travelling through South America. He had boarded the bus in Embarcación with the intention of travelling all the way east along

Highway 81 to Formosa, a journey that passes through Juárez. He hadn't sufficient local currency to do that and was not allowed to pay the fare in a mix of Argentine and Paraguayan money. So he got off in Juárez and had breakfast with us while the drivers did the same in a café, and we changed his Paraguayan *guaraníes* into Argentine currency for him to continue his journey.

Special and much anticipated visitors each year were the Translation Consultants of the United Bible Societies, come to help the Wichi translation project and encourage us. One person much involved now in promoting the Wichi language and its Bible visited us when we were living in Misión La Paz. He turned up like an apparition in that remote village wearing a large hat, speaking English and introducing himself as Chris Wallis, a British anthropologist working in the Paraguayan Chaco across the River Pilcomayo. He had heard there were British missionaries on the Argentine side and had crossed the river in the rickety cable-car to meet us. Though he was not a Christian, we appreciated this totally unexpected visit, enjoyed talking with him and found him a bed for the night.

More than ten years passed before we met again. He arrived in Juárez with our Argentine friend and colleague Helena Oliver, who burst out laughing when I asked her what plans she had. She answered that she and Chris were to be married! We were surprised by joy. We had heard they had been members of a team tasked by the Anglican Church of Paraguay with evaluating the social projects there. We had heard that Chris had had a genuine spiritual awakening and now followed Christ, but we had not heard their matrimonial news!

On my 2011 visit to Argentina I spent a week with Chris and Helena in their very humble home in the Wichi village of Santa María, whose former indigenous pastor, the late Zebedeo Torres, had led Helena to faith in Christ many years before. I reminded Chris of that evening back in early 1979 when he first encountered us in Misión La Paz, and asked him what he thought of us. "Ah", he replied, "I thought, 'These missionaries have good intentions, but they really don't know what they're doing.'"

Then, with a twinkle in his eye, he added, "I've since changed my mind!"

17
God is with us

The story of Helena and Chris warmed our hearts as we saw the Father-heart of God express itself in our own and others' experience during our years in northern Argentina.

Bishop David preached one morning at San Andrés church in Salta when we were visiting the city. During his sermon on John 5, he pointed out that *"las coincidencias son los milagros en que Dios no quiere aparecer"* ("coincidences are miracles in which God wishes not to appear"). He recounted an up-to-date incident regarding Helena and a flight she'd made to the UK via Paris. A friend had arrived late at her point of departure, Salta airport, with some letters for her to take for folk in England, but a representative of the airline, Aerolíneas Argentinas, kindly took them on to the plane for her. The stewardess then called Helena's name and destination over the plane's public address asking her to collect them, whereupon a passenger called to her and said he worked for the Argentine Embassy in Paris. He proved an ideal contact because she had to collect her passport from the French Consulate as she passed through Buenos Aires and was uneasy about crossing Paris. She arrived safely in England and phoned David with the wonderful story.

The building in which we listened to that sermon had had a quietly miraculous beginning as a house of God. As the members looked for a new place to rent somewhere in Salta, a missionary driving around spotted the building and contacted an Argentine lay leader of the congregation, saying, "Come on, I want to take you to a place where I think the church can meet". The man replied, "I know already where it is. God has told me, so *I'll take you.*" And he drove the missionary across the city to the same place.

God in Juárez
One day in Juárez Margaret called at a local shop owned by an irascible

alcoholic and his never over-friendly wife. That day the woman surprised Margaret saying she wanted to accept Christ and follow him. They had been to a witchdoctor about the husband's problem. Margaret went home to get some literature in Spanish recently sent her from London, and just at that moment a colleague from Embarcación arrived and produced a helpful Gospel tract from his luggage. We took it to her, rejoicing at such divine timing.

Another woman came seeking a Bible; her husband had burned her first one and thrown her second one down their long-drop. She left him, preferring God's Word as a partner.

On our tenth wedding anniversary we decided to try out the latest small café to open in Juárez. We found the place empty of customers and the owner particularly glad to see us. Dispirited by issues in life, he welcomed us with a good snack and shared his problems, gladly listening to our words about Christ and bowing his head in prayer with us.

I preached often, perhaps too often, and one Saturday preparing a sermon for the Wichi in Barrio Pilcomayo next morning, I prayed for a decent-sized congregation. Immediately the wife of the lay leader of another Wichi community appeared at my window to ask me to take a service there next morning. I said I couldn't but would pick them all up in my truck and take them to Barrio Pilcomayo for a joint service. This I did and the church was full.

Another day a young Toba leader came to tell me his dilemma. He wanted to go to Bible School in Misión Chaqueña but the Juárez town council would not allow him leave from his job as a tractor driver. We prayed together and afterwards he said he was going to Bible School as he felt that was what God wanted. Months later he came smiling to my door to tell me God had answered our prayers; he had been to Bible School and the council had changed its mind and allowed him to resume his work as a tractor driver.

A wing (problem) and a prayer

The head of the Bible Society of Argentina, with which we have an excellent relationship, humorously suggested one time that the Anglican Church must pray more than the Bible Societies. Very unlikely, but his comment was prompted by the arrival of a long-awaited piece of computer hardware for the Wichi translation project, provided by the United Bible Societies (UBS) in Miami. A worker from there was taking it to Chile from where it would somehow reach me in due course. But when the plane made its scheduled stop in Buenos Aires, a wing problem delayed the continuation of the flight by six hours. On hearing this, the head of the Bible Society of Argentina dashed to the airport to pick it up then rush it across to the unsuspecting Bishop David who he knew happened to be waiting at the other main airport for a flight back north to Salta! A wing and a prayer indeed.

Getting equipment such as computer hardware across borders was a nerve-wracking issue which required prayerfulness. I received a new computer at a training course in Asunción, Paraguay, in 1989 and stayed an extra couple of days so that the representative of the UBS, a Chilean lady, could accompany me across the frontier into Argentina. When we reached the border she simply walked across with the new machine, right down the middle of the road. I followed with my old one, and no one challenged us.

I thanked the lady and the Lord, bade her farewell and continued my journey by bus. However, I had forgotten there was an Argentine frontier police post a short way on. Here all passengers had to alight and my heart sank as an inquisitive young gendarme took my bag out of the hold and opened it; it was the one containing my old computer and equipment. He looked suspiciously towards an older colleague; however, this one was surprisingly friendly and showed a positive interest on seeing 'Sociedad Bíblica Argentina' on a document. "Adelante, señor", he said, still smiling ("You may continue, sir"). My new computer was still on the bus, looking innocent and innocuous in its case!

18
Trámites - or Termites?

Crossing borders, internationally or provincially, was no one's favourite experience. In 1987 we travelled home to the UK via Paraguay but were fined forty dollars on leaving that country because their colleagues at the Argentina-Paraguay border had not stamped our passports when we entered days before. Alison cried out, *"¡No nos van a dejar pasar!"* ("They're not going to let us through!"). Fortunately, we had forty dollars, which was a lot of money to us at the time. On hearing the story in England a kind lady sent us a cheque to cover it.

On another occasion the Paraguayans fined me a certain amount for crossing the land border into their country on my Argentine identity document rather than my passport, even though that was normal practice. "Do you know why they do that?" asked an Argentine colleague. "To get money." As he was well aware, the Argentine authorities could be just as perverse and obstructive.

When I first arrived in Argentina in 1977, Bishop Patrick sent me to the Registry Office in Salta to start the process of getting my ID. Such processes were known as *trámites*, and he told me to my surprise that this one would probably take a year! It did, after numerous visits to numerous government offices, police stations and hospitals with numerous forms to be completed by numerous officials and the taking of numerous fingerprints. Once done, I could start the *trámite* for my second ID …

The key to an eventual visa

For our daughter Alison who was born during our 1980 UK leave, we had to get her IDs when we returned to Argentina. Because she needed a permanent visa, the *trámites* started one step back. It began ominously and comically. On the way to start the process, while waiting for a bus I heard a call from a man at a second-floor window who had locked himself in and was shouting to me to call the doorkeeper of the block of flats.

I couldn't get in the main door, nor could I see the doorman and so he suggested I get the keys out of his car. He threw down his car keys, I opened the car and found his house keys. I then had to throw them up, but the first throw struck cables and rebounded. The second fell just short and landed on the balcony over the entrance. To try to retrieve them I rang the bell of the lady whose flat opened on to the balcony, but she was out. Then I threw up the car keys, but the man missed them and they dropped on to the balcony beside the other keys. A woman came out of the main door and so I slipped in to look for the doorman, but just missed him as he passed in the lift. Finally he came out and I explained the situation. He called the woman next door to the balcony, she retrieved the keys with a broom, went up and unlocked the man from his flat. He came down, unlocked his car, and gratefully gave me a lift – by this time I'd missed two or three buses and a passing colleague.

It shouldn't happen to a baby

I began the *trámite* with a visit to the Ministry of Social Wellbeing to get forms for Alison's medical card, while Margaret took her to another centre where the technicians refused to take the blood of a baby. After breakfast with the bishop's wife, in whose home Alison had now fallen asleep, Margaret returned to the centre and on arrival found the doctor had already filled in the form for the blood analysis and urine without even seeing Alison. We then went to the Children's Hospital to have her chest x-rayed. She screamed. Off before dawn next day to the San Bernardo Hospital where we waited an age for Alison to have her eyes tested. Eventually Margaret pushed her way forward, pointing out how Alison was screaming from tiredness. The nurse took the forms, the doctor looked at one eye and said, *"¡Qué hermosos los ojos!"* ("What lovely eyes!") and signed the form. Margaret then took the bus to the frontier police station to get a written consent to begin the *trámite*. They said they didn't need to see Alison until she was ten, but gave her the consent when Margaret showed

77

them an order from Immigration for us to get one.

Five days later we were off again to the Ministry to obtain the medical card, Alison entertaining folk in the waiting-room for over an hour. Then to Immigration to hand over innumerable forms, certificates, photocopies – only to be told we needed more. We protested to no avail. So next day we went to the pink police station where I managed to persuade an officer to let me dictate the authorisation, which I then signed and he stamped and countersigned. Then I got birth certificate and translation photocopied, then went to the bank to pay for the *trámite*, then back to Immigration where I got through, with a little word from the person I saw the day before, to a lady who gathered together the many papers and prepared to start the *trámite*. Two months on Alison finally had her permanent visa after notification from the police was delivered to the bishop. We had to pick it up in Salta; had we been delayed getting there from the interior, we may have had to endure the whole procedure again as we were given only five days' notice to collect the document! Then it was the start of the *trámite* at the Registry Office to see which documents Alison required for her ID. There were many and I won't bore you with the saga. Sometimes we felt *trámites* would be better known as termites for the way they ate away at our time and our mental state. But I *will* mention Elisabeth's (sorry, Elizabeth's) identity document.

You can't call her that – it's not in the book

Our second daughter was born in our home in Tartagal, delivered by our neighbour, missionary and midwife Margaret Grebby. That night Argentine missionary doctor Manolo Jurczuk came to visit and wrote out the birth certificate. She was to be Elisabeth Juana – known as Elisabeth Jane, but foreign names were not allowed in those days of the military dictatorship, so the Spanish equivalent of 'Jane' would have to appear on her ID.

A week later I went to buy the special stamps to set in motion the *trámite* for her ID and took them to the Registry Office, but it was busy so I returned home. Next day I had another fruitless wait there. When

78

the boss saw me leaving she called and said she'd attend to me "*en seguida*"; but although that means 'straight away' I'd learned over my years in Argentina, where time matters less than here, that it could be anything from minutes to hours. So I returned home again. Five days later I went back to the Registry Office at 7:25am and was there an hour. When I was finally attended to, the girl at the desk told me the birth certificate was not valid – something to do with the signatures of the witnesses, I think. But before I could protest, the boss called her into a corner and whispered something to her, presumably that I'd been there twice before. So, bureaucracy was overruled and the *trámite* began – but having entered as father of a daughter called Elisabeth, I came out with one called Elizabeth. The latter spelling was the correct one, I was told, as it was the one in the official book of permissible names and spellings. The government wouldn't allow 'Elisabeth' any more than 'Jane'.

And despite the trauma of those days, I think she, and we, are glad she carries the more common version, 'Elizabeth'!

Living Juárez: author with local folk

Author and Margaret in UK

19
A night on the rails

The waiting-room

My first experience of Argentine railways had come at the beginning of 1978 when I sat on the station of Padre Lozano, a few miles from Misión Chaqueña, with Assistant Bishop Mario waiting for a train to Juárez where he lived. It was the 7:20pm and in the time before its arrival at 9:30 we had the chance to talk with the bored and lonely stationmaster. "Juárez …. Juárrrez", he kept repeating after ascertaining where we were headed; either the name had a certain musicality for him or it offered the opportunity to while away a few more seconds. "Train should be here anytime", he said unhelpfully, before adding, even more so, "I hope it doesn't derail. It did last week. It was in the papers. Look, I'll show you how it happened. Just up the line." He proceeded to give us a spontaneous demonstration of this event, which "happens from time to time, you know."

Moments of silence, then the subject of conversation suddenly changed. "You two are brothers?" he asked. The question nonplussed me. I looked at the dark-skinned bishop against my own pale skin and ginger locks – before realising he meant 'Brothers' with a capital B – or 'Brethren', members of that Christian denomination.

"No", I replied, "we belong to the Anglican Church." "Ah, the Anglican Church", he responded. "I like the Anglican Church. Do you know what I like about the Anglican Church? It forbids everything. Drinking, smoking, dancing. You can't do anything if you're an Anglican. I like a church like that."

"I wish it would forbid train delays", I mused uncharitably, before we explained that there were other things about Anglicanism, other more positive things, shall we say.

On the way at last

Finally, at 9:30 the 7:20 was approaching, and another passenger turned up – a swarthy old man with a heavily lined face and one eye who must have seen, or half-seen, a few things in his Chaco lifetime. I wondered if he'd lost his other eye hunting trains. But this sudden upsurge of support for the railways led the stationmaster to don his shirt and become the ticket clerk as he conducted our eager threesome into an office where, in murky Dickensian surroundings, he proceeded to compile our tickets by the light of a disinterested kerosene lamp. Calling the bishop and me first, he wrote in the details, asking us where we were going – he was obviously not blessed with a good memory – before stamping the tickets, duplicating them, looking at the back, checking the front, writing in something else, making sure we were *both* going to Juárez, and collecting the cash. "You might get a seat" were his final sterling words of encouragement. Then a cry, a vulture soared away and "Here comes the machine", exclaimed the bishop. So we scaled a carriage and I sat on my case, not bold enough to ask any of the snoozing, snoring, sprawling passengers to shove up. We set off into the Chaco night, the adjacent coaches swaying fearfully and an official giving himself an electric shock repairing a light.

"Hey, youth! Don't drop off to sleep or you'll drop off the train", a woman advised a fellow sprawled in the passage behind me next to the empty outside.

"Hey, old man! Be careful of that gap between the carriages", someone exclaimed as our one-eyed companion staggered from his seat to disembark at the first stop.

As the train shuddered to a halt, I moved along and installed myself in his seat before the person adjacent, a young lady looking strikingly attractive and splendidly indignant, could sprawl over both. Whether it was the latter sentiment or simply a few troublesome insects that provoked her to strike my ear with a rolled-up magazine five minutes later is debatable. However, the magazine, unfurled on her lap, revealed a Roman Catholic article entitled (in translation) "Let us evangelise the world", so maybe I was a beneficiary of a new global system of proselytisation. Some time later, having apparently dozed off, I came round with a start, having collapsed into the young lady. I braced myself for another manifestation of fly-swatting evangelism, but she was asleep and I was 'saved'.

Finally, at 4:30am the train arrived in Juárez and we emerged from the grunt and sweat of a weary Chaco journey. Bishop Mario gave me a bed for a couple of hours, then produced a wheelbarrow and three boys. He placed my heavy case on it, bade the boys get shoving and me goodbye for now, and our new 'train' set off for the Mission.

20
Training for mission?

Margaret and I got to know each other on another extremely long train journey on a hot December day in 1978. She had had her own experience of trains as a single woman travelling alone on holiday through Bolivia a year or two earlier. She was advised by the ticket-inspector on the train that she would need a visa in Santa Cruz, which left her momentarily nonplussed. "Don't worry", said a young man in the carriage, "you can stay the night with me and my family". "Yes", echoed other passengers, "you'll be all right. They're a good family."

So Margaret stayed with the strangers, who gave her excellent hospitality, and continued her journey by bus the next night. She chose to do that stage of her trip nocturnally to avoid seeing the steep drops to the side of the narrow, winding, mountainous road. She forgot, however, to check the moon's phases: it was full moon and everything showed up!

Train spotting

Trains were to give us many other memories once we settled in Juárez, which was situated on the long straight line built in the 1930s stretching from Embarcación in the west to Formosa in the east. When they ran to time they were helpful, especially in the rainy season when the parallel Highway 81, mostly dirt road, was often impassable. There was the *ferrobús*, which was a two-carriage railcar, the *pasajero* (passenger train), the *carguero* (goods train) and the *petrolero* (fuel-carrying train), and we and our colleagues had experience of them all. But they didn't always obey the timetable …

The ferrobús ran for a time and had its adventures. One time it had only one gear – reverse – so its journeys were, so to speak, all return trips. Another time it was off the rails, literally, when its drunken driver ignored a signal and ploughed into a goods train, injuring forty people.

The passenger train was then thankfully reinstated and a carnival atmosphere welcomed its first arrival at the station in Juárez. But it rarely delivered what it promised. One morning at 2am I took a visiting colleague to the station for her return journey to Embarcación and Salta, but after a wait we were advised that it would be coming in 24 hours. "Go home and sleep well; tomorrow you'll have a train", said the pastorally-minded but deeply irksome station employee. At least she did get away next early morning.

One night I took another visiting colleague to the station for her journey, and lo, the train came in. I saw her on to it and went home. I later learned that it sat in the station until 6am. Two early mornings later at 1:15am I rushed five indians to the station and they apparently sat on the train for three hours until it left. Two colleagues, meantime, boarded a goods train in Embarcación at 3pm and didn't arrive in Juárez until 2pm next day after the driver stopped in Morillo, where he presumably lived, and went to bed.

Training bishops

Our new bishop, Maurice Sinclair, earned the nickname *Pelhaywo* (Rain-man) from the Wichi because whenever and however he travelled in his first weeks, it rained and he often got stuck. The most dramatic experience was when he terminated a visit to Juárez early because the rains prevented him travelling to the indian villages, so he left his truck with us and opted for the *pasajero*. He ended up staying six hours longer than planned, however, because that was the length of time he was on the station waiting for the 1:30am which arrived at 7:30. It then derailed along the way when a bridge collapsed and the line flooded. Some folk climbed on to the train roof to escape the water and a colleague who'd heard about the incident managed to drive from Embarcación to the rescue of Maurice and the colleague travelling with him.

One of Maurice's successors, the current diocesan bishop, Nick Drayson, came to visit in his pre-episcopal days and arrived on a *petrolero*. We'd waited for him on three buses and one passenger train until he finally came waving to us from the guard's van of the fuel-train. He'd been two nights on the way from Formosa, having set off by bus until the road became impassable. He'd then survived 8½ hours on the *petrolero*.

Bog-standard start to holiday of our lives

Finally, there was our special Argentine holiday as a family in 1991.

Holidays usually happened in midsummer which was also the heart of the rainy season. We should have heeded the wisdom of *criollo* pastor Mario who told us that if the local greengrocer known as Míster didn't get in with his lorry-load of fruit and vegetables, it wouldn't be worth our trying to get out by road.

But Assistant Bishop Mario's driver thought vehicles *were* getting in, so we decided to try, using that truck of Bishop Maurice that he'd abandoned in Juárez before his perilous train journey. So we set off at 8:30am, Mario's driver at the wheel, but at the provincial border the frontier policeman said no vehicle had got in and the road was reportedly cut at the little town of Pagé. However, we continued to there and found a lorry in the ditch; it was full of pigs, who I guess were in their element.

We managed to negotiate our way through the mud between this lorry and another and were glad of the experience of the Embarcación ambulance driver who was travelling with us together with his wife and baby. Beyond Pagé we were told by an approaching truck that we wouldn't get through a stretch of water beyond the town of Los Blancos. We reached there but soon came across Míster's lorry in the ditch, while his tractor, a pick-up truck and the 1935 Chevrolet lorry from Los Blancos endeavoured to pull him out. We tried to get through but became stuck, and after insistent advice from one of the men *(Les digo la verdad, no van a pasar* "I'm telling you straight, you won't get through"), we took the decision to turn back. The tractor eventually pulled Míster out, then us, and we turned round. It rescued us then from another bog and we got back to Los Blancos where the Roman Catholic nun welcomed us warmly, fed us and looked after us very well.

An evening in the guard's van

At 3pm we went to the station and waited for an expected *petrolero*, which came at 6:30 after Elizabeth had burned her ear on the rail listening for its approach. The stationmaster was a glass-half-empty man: "It might not come; and if it does come, it might not stop; and if it does stop, it might not take you."

But it did all three and we clambered into the guard's van and headed for the next station, Morillo. There was doubt as to whether there were staff to go further, but after an hour and forty minutes we were on our way once more. We paid the passenger train fare, though the guard was another without a degree in mathematics: *"¿Cuántos son ustedes?" "Dos adultos y dos chicas." "Cuántos en total?"* ("How many are you?" "Two adults and two children." "How many in total?")

When rain started he invited us inside his van with its smelly toilet and no light, but we were glad of anything. Rain was still falling when we finally reached Embarcación at 3am and waded through the lake-like streets to the Mission, guided by the ambulance driver who lived opposite. At the last minute back home I'd chosen to take a large shoulder-bag instead of a case, an inspired decision.

The first and most dramatic stage of our holiday had been completed. We travelled to Salta later that day and then headed south, travelling thousands of miles overland seeing wonderful sights over the next three weeks and enjoying what was truly the holiday of our lives. But honestly, there's nothing so special as getting stuck in the Chaco and spending Sunday evening in the smelly guard's van of a *petrolero*!

21
Coaching for mission?

Those thousands of miles of our holiday were spent on Argentina's excellent coach network, most of which uses tarmac roads. We slept, ate and relaxed on the buses, and in later years when I visited the country twice-yearly from the UK I preferred to travel from Buenos Aires to the north and back terrestrially. It took 24 hours – and sometimes delays extended that – but I also found it left me relaxed for the work ahead or the flight back to the UK.

But as our 1991 holiday had started in mud, it ended in dust. After that huge mileage across Argentina, we soon knew we were back on the last leg of our journey home. One look at the bus that we boarded in Formosa told us we'd shortly be back in the sticks – no air-conditioning, no toilet, no video, no coffee-bar, and when we arrived in Juárez our luggage in the hold was covered in dust. And so were we.

Why do you need a timetable?
The buses in the Chaco were usually elderly and unreliable as to working and time. On one occasion we had a visitor from the small Chorote indigenous group, pastor and New Testament translator Julián Gómez, come from Misión La Paz by bus and train. His journey back home had a bad start. I rose at 3am to run him to the bus-station in Juárez for a bus to Embarcación that didn't appear. No one knew anything about it but the sign said it existed. So I brought him back home, and at 8am Margaret and caretaker Emilio went to try to clarify the situation. They were told there was a nightwatchman who knew everything, and when located he said the bus had gone at 10:30pm last night, its 'normal' time. Margaret was unimpressed (understatement) and asked him why he left the 3am sign there. "Well", he replied in surprise, "they can always ask *me*."

We found another way for Julián to 'escape' later that day. But Margaret's reaction must have stirred the nightwatchman because when we got to the bus station with Julián, the misleading sign had been covered up. This time his bus arrived and left on schedule.

Night on the pews

One Saturday morning when the family were away in Salta, I rose early to go with Bishop Mario in his truck to the town of Las Lomitas for the church anniversary festivities in one of the Wichi neighbourhoods, Chacra 27. But he sent a message to say his truck had a problem and he wasn't going. So I took the 8:30am bus and arrived just after midday to be regaled as a hero for coming – though the bishop was less popular. I spent an enjoyable afternoon with the church folk and intended to return to Juárez on the 5:30pm bus in time to fulfil a preaching engagement late that night in the Centre Church. But a storm broke forcing a change of plan which meant sleeping in the Chacra 27 church on two hard benches pushed together, with sheets provided by the layman-in-charge.

Next morning, Sunday, there was a service with visitors arriving from other neighbourhoods, but it began so late there wasn't time for Communion. It ended abruptly and I was whisked off to another stew, then to the road to await the early afternoon bus. But it didn't turn up and after nearly two hours I walked back to Chacra 27 in the hot sun. At 5pm the layman-in-charge accompanied me to the stop for the next bus, but after two more hours I gave up again and walked into town to the bus-station where I found it broken down. The relief bus finally turned up at 10pm but didn't leave until 11:40 because a tyre needed repair. I finally reached home at 3:10am and rose at 7:30 to meet the family off the overnight bus from Salta. They'd frozen because the air-conditioning was on, but eventually Margaret, again unimpressed, persuaded them to turn it off.

Chasing buses …

… was not unknown. I chased one through Juárez one night so a visitor could catch it, only to find that rain in Las Lomitas meant it wasn't going anywhere. I was due to travel in the other direction on the 3am bus to Embarcación (it did exist at that time) and Margaret drove to the bus-station at 11:30pm to check if it would be going. She returned in haste to say it was leaving at midnight to try to beat the next rain! It suited our visitor so we woke him and just made it.

On the way we hit stretches of mud and also spent three hours in Los Blancos, presumably to realign with the timetable. The whole journey took nearly twelve hours, about three times as long as in normal circumstances. But what was normal?

22

"History is more or less bunk" (Henry Ford) – and some of your vehicles too, Henry

I can still recall Bishop David telling me with a smile at the start of our final term of service that rather than the diocese getting us a new pick-up, we could have his Ford now that he'd replaced it with a newer model. After all, it was well suited to the challenges of Chaco roads and had two cabins so could take a family and other passengers comfortably as well as plenty of luggage.

I should have realised that some things are not quite as promising as they seem. We were in the city of Salta and so was the truck, but as I was then not accustomed to this size of vehicle, arrangements were made for our colleague Helena to drive us north to Embarcación and then for the curiously named Zósimo, a cheerful old Wichi friend and experienced driver, to do the second, mainly dirt-road, section to Juárez.

We left with Helena at 7:20 on a wet Saturday morning and the truck 'danced' on the tarmac. We stopped to put air in the tyres to even the pressures and reached Embarcación safely but slightly concerned. Then even on the dirt road the truck continued its ballroom routine, prompting Zósimo to describe it as *w'oknaj* (drunk). We stopped in Los Blancos where we found the rear tyres hot. He did a repair on the brake linings and we finally arrived safely in Juárez nearly twelve hours after leaving Salta, just as rain began to fall and two rainbows appeared in the northern sky: portents of a happy and fruitful final three-and-a-half years of ministry to come – though not, alas, of trouble-free motoring.

A breakdown of the Ford's career
We both soon got used to driving the Ford and the adventures piled up.

91

At one point a succession of breakdowns led to the need for a complete rebore, identified by the mechanic who lived opposite us, a decent man who worked hard with mixed results to keep the vehicle on the road. The rebore had to be done in Salta so Bishop David took the engine there on his return from a visit to Juárez and ten days later it reappeared - on the bus. I somehow collected it and the mechanic reinstalled it. The next week I happened to be in a café in town when a man called to me and announced with a proud smile that he was the bus driver who'd brought my *motor* from Salta.

It might have had a rebore but it never left us bored – just frustrated and occasionally frightened. One day Margaret and a colleague found it accelerating of its own accord with braking useless, but she somehow managed to pull up at the mechanic's and he identified a broken part. Shortly afterwards a local family bravely borrowed it for a Sunday School outing along a stony road to a village to the north and arrived back with no brakes. The mechanic repaired the brake-pipe, probably broken by a stone thrown up by the wheels. On returning from our next trip as a family to visit the communities to the north, the brakes again failed and I had to drive carefully around town to drop off a policeman who'd thumbed a lift with us – it was always politic as well as polite to pick up police – and then get us all home. We headed alarmingly towards our house fence but thankfully the Ford stopped two metres short, to great whoops of laughter and joy from Alison and Elizabeth and sighs of relief from mum and dad.

The brakes were repaired next day but when I set off on my next journey I found only one gear – reverse. So I drove back, literally, to the mechanic, glad he lived near. This was fixed and it was fine – except that it then started to jump out of gear. So the mechanic examined it and discovered another part was needed, which he said he would install gratis.

Don't promise what you can't deliver
A representative of SAMS visited us and I proudly presented to him the programme I'd prepared for his three days with us. The heart of it

was a visit to the Wichi communities of Potrillo to the north, taking with us our nurse colleague Beryl whose other ministry was Christian education by extension.

We set off for the day trip but were back by midday after the engine consistently lost power – all due, it was thought, to a screw not properly tightened when the air-filter had been cleaned in readiness for the trip. One small screw created one big disappointment. At least our visitor was made aware of the trials of travel in the Chaco – and was back in time to take a trip with our neighbour Chris Hawksbee who was off to a well-drilling. So he got some experience of life in the village communities.

Soon afterwards another mechanic, not always sober, repaired the doors, thus enabling us to get in and out. Then an ignition problem meant that for a time we had to start the truck by putting two wires together under the steering column, then turning the ignition. To stop the engine we separated the wires.

Petrol was not always available in Juárez, especially in the rainy season when the tankers couldn't get through. But one time we heard it had arrived and I drove to the petrol station to get my 20-litre ration, only to lose most of it almost immediately because the joint on the tank had worked loose. Soon afterwards it had another leak when Margaret was driving through town, so she left it parked and the mechanic fetched it next day and did his latest repair – followed by an even later one the following day – then a latest one when smoke came out of the engine – then an even later latest one when it broke down with another gearbox problem.

It spent two Christmases away, stuck at the Centre Church one year and outside Pastor Mario's house another because of sudden storms. One of those Christmas Days ended with me digging it out and getting it back home; the other time I found it no longer stuck - but it wouldn't start.

Green tea and Poxipol

So you ask: did it ever work? Did we ever get from A to B successfully?

Absolutely! For our winter holiday in July 1989 we travelled hundreds of miles along mainly dirt roads with no hint of a problem, not even a puncture, as we visited many Wichi communities along the River Pilcomayo. It was a wonderful time and our Wichi friend Corino, who came as assistant in case of truck problems, had an unexpectedly easy ride and was able to preach in some of the churches we visited.

We invited him next year – when it turned out altogether different. Or perhaps one should say, altogether back to normal. The problems began early. Just past Fraga, the first town west from Juárez, the radiator sprang a leak. A passing eastbound motorist – there were few other vehicles on that lonely highway – tried unsuccessfully to bung it with green tea, so drove on to Fraga to notify the frontier police. An hour or so later the truck belonging to the Roman Catholic priest from Juárez came out from Fraga where he was attending a fiesta for the Virgin of Fraga. The two men in it towed us back there, then a young man closed up the burst part and added *Poxipol* adhesive. We were given empanadas and Coca-Cola from the fiesta, watched folk we knew arrive from Juárez, and witnessed a drunken fight.

At 3pm we were on our way but at Los Blancos the engine again overheated, and so at Morillo we stopped at a garage where the mechanic cleaned and soldered the radiator. We finally arrived in Tartagal at 9:45pm where we were to spend a few days before heading to the Pilcomayo villages. The truck's reputation had gone before it and our friend José Cicka had booked it into a good garage where it was repaired over the next days with new brake linings, new radiator, attention to steering and gears, new shock-absorbers etc. etc. The bill was large and we hadn't the money to hand until the diocesan finance department in Salta could send it. But the mechanic accepted a third of it and was happy to wait for the rest. The radiator salesman also agreed to delayed payment because *"confío en los evangelistas"* ("I trust the evangelists" – he meant the evangelicals). But this overhaul did it good and we had only minor problems on the rest of the long trip.

So that was the Ford. On our last day in charge of it in 1991 it ran out of petrol. We'd hoped it would last. Then Elizabeth and her little Toba friend Rosalina in an hour of naughty play removed the buttons from the upholstered roof. It somehow all seemed fitting. But at least the Ford's engine never caught fire, as that of our earlier Fiat did, and for that we were grateful. I think.

The infamous Ford! Alison safe up the tree!

Stuck! Muddy start to a holiday

Transport to conference

Packed church for Bible launch

23
What's in a nickname?

Long before those adventures in Juárez, and during my two months in Misión La Paz early in 1979 when I got to know Margaret and also made strides forward with the Wichi language, I embarked upon a memorable journey to the village of Santa María, further upriver on the Pilcomayo, with colleague Dick Hines and his wife Jen.

The Wichi like to give nicknames to missionaries and Dick's was *Tsileklek*, a species of hawk. I was also named after a bird, *Ifwalalä*, the vermilion flycatcher, because of my hair colour. Other names given to missionaries included *Tson'ataj (Sheep)* for one whose cough made him sound like a sheep, *Tiyäjphämtes (Jumper)*, for one who always looked as if he was walking through long grass, and *Kato T'unho (Stiff Elbow)* given humorously to a much loved pioneer on account of his elbow becoming rigid when the scales on which he weighed out things like rice and sugar in the mission store reached the very exact amount – not a grain or granule more! The equally loved Bishop Patrick Harris was *Käjyentes,* the one who makes us happy, because of his demeanour and ministry. There were the more obvious *Pites* and *Piteya* (Tall Man and Tall Woman) given to other deeply loved long-serving missionaries.

Taking the waters at Pozo Mosquito

Dick Hines would soon be my best man, but on the occasion recorded here he was leading our expedition into the further interior in his Ford pick-up. Yes, it was a Ford! Dusk was falling as we reached a narrow valley that had filled with rainwater during this wet season. Our Wichi guide disembarked, splashed his way to the other side and signalled to Dick that it was safe to cross. Dick revved the engine, slammed it into second gear and asked Jen to remind him, once across, that he'd got the choke out. And off we went. It was one of those resplendent Chaco nights as the near-full moon set itself to listen in on traditional missionary travel talk as the vehicle slipped inexorably into a hole: "Everybody out and everybody off the back!" "Push from the front first!" "Be easier without these wretched mosquitoes!" "We can fix the winch to that *algarrobo* tree." "Wouldn't it be quicker to send one of these chaps on bike to Santa Victoria to get a tractor to pull us out?" "*N'ahut!* Push! Heave! Shove!" "We've got spectators."

Spectators? In the distance two *criollo* horsemen in white shirts under a white moon stared at our plight, phantasmal against the bewitchingly dark forest background. Probably wondering who these fools were, stuck in a hole. "Should stick to horses." But they just gazed in silence while we grunted and heaved and the winch creaked and the engine misfired, having had enough of the day and the trip. We and our passengers were, it seemed, condemned, those passengers all being Wichi – our guide, a woman with learning difficulties, several folk being ferried (ill-chosen word) to the doctor's surgery in Santa Victoria, and another woman who was nine-months pregnant.

"Ever wondered what we're doing out here?" asked Dick as I stood by the rear wheels, water squelching through my wellingtons, heaving with the other men – and almost heaving in another sense against the exhaust fumes in the moment before the engine cut out, against the pregnant woman's vomit trailing across the open back of the truck, and against the roll of my own stomach, empty for thirteen hours because to have eaten in front of the very poor people of Pozo Toro village, whom we'd visited earlier in the day, would have been improper. Meanwhile, the mosquitoes got on with *their* meal.

Suddenly we found ourselves serenaded. The cowboys on their horses were going on their way, singing their traditional songs of solitude and melancholy as they disappeared into the forest. For us, after a coffee break, it was back to straining and heaving, and at 1:30am, after four hours' work, the Ford was hauled clear of the water, and lo, she fired. "Just a little help from the Lord at the end of a long day", mused Dick – and I think he remembered to put the choke in. Jen cooked spaghetti over a fire and with tins of meat paste and sardines we and our long-suffering but stoical passengers fortified ourselves under the Southern Cross and the majestic plethora of stars of the Milky Way.

And so to camp-bed.

After four hours' sleep we prepared ourselves for the rest of our journey, reflecting on our nocturnal experience, when suddenly an exclamation from Dick pierced the silence: "Stone the crows!" "What is it?" we asked. "Look over there", he said, pointing to a piece of ground twenty yards away just lit by the rising sun. "We could have crossed there … there's not a drop of water … stone the crows!"

24
Celebrating, Living

On a bus one day the *criollo* lady next to me asked if evangelicals celebrate Christmas! We certainly have fond memories of Christmases and other festivals enjoyed with the indians, who went out of their way to invite and welcome us.

Our first Christmas in Juárez was a rainy one and it took us 50 minutes to walk the muddy, watery mile to Barrio Pilcomayo for morning service. Afterwards traditional stews were cooked in huge pans, while the wonderful Christian leader Isabel (later Rev) and her sister Melita made empanadas and someone barbecued a goat. We ate at 2:00pm under a tree and someone arrived with a wheelbarrow of crates of fizzy drinks and ice. A similar feast took place at New Year, together with locally grown watermelon, coffee, then tug-o-war with the women usually beating the men.

Another Christmas morning we went early to the main Wichi neighbourhood, Barrio Obrero, because the pastor had told me the service would begin between 7:30 and 8am. It didn't begin until 9 so we waited next door in the empty house of Beryl who was on UK leave, and found her cat locked in since the last visitor was there five days before. Alison and Elizabeth had the Christmas Day surprise of finding two newborn kittens in a box. We then went to lunch with the Toba people in their neighbourhood, eating meat that tasted off, before heading to Barrio Pilcomayo for empanadas and fizzy drinks.

Three Indian communities on one Christmas Day – we were living Juárez.

The following year after service we walked to Isabel's house for Christmas lunch and found a large crowd there. We'd bought a goat which, together with a pig, was cooked in a mud-brick oven built by a good Wichi friend from Misión La Paz. A long wait was survived until at 2:30pm I was asked if I had a word before we ate! I hadn't (though sounds were emanating from my stomach), so Isidro was called upon and spoke for ten minutes from Isaiah 9!

The food was delicious, with stew, *pan dulce* (the local Christmas cake) and watermelon to boot. After tug-o-war, I recited Alison and Elizabeth's story of Horace the Bear, transposed into a Wichi setting with Horace eating Isabel, Isidro and other Wichi friends in the forest! The indians enjoyed such buffoonery.

As far as our *criollo* friends were concerned, it was more often a case of individual invitations from and to them for meals, something greatly enjoyed. But when our departure came in July 1991 they made a big party for us in our garden. Many friends from church came along, together with our local baker, shopkeepers, some of the girls' schoolfriends and their parents, translator Isidro and his wife, and the former mayor. There was food aplenty and an enormous cake, and leftovers were handed out at church later. Somehow it confirmed that we had not just 'survived' Juárez, we had truly 'lived' it.

"The most humble of all missionary houses"

Such was the description of our home in Juárez by a new SAMS staff member who was visiting the missionaries across the different republics. I have earlier (chapter 2) made mention of its whitewashed mud-brick structure, zinc roof panels, false ceiling of polystyrene and floors of earth or tiles. For an office Isidro and I worked in a hut in the garden where we could be separate from the goings-on in the house. Our long-serving home-help Catalina, a *criolla*, used to walk from her house on six afternoons a week, often in scorching temperatures, to clean and wash for us. The compound was at one end of the town, not as convenient for shops and churches as it could have been, but it was very much home. Another house for *señoritas* stood opposite.

Such houses were vulnerable to creepy-crawlies, not all of the benevolent kind, and one annual activity was fumigation by the 'anti-chagas' men to get rid of *vinchucas*, sinister black bugs which can infect a person with a form of sleeping-sickness called *chagas*. Mosquito-nets were essential to combat *vinchucas* as well as mosquitoes, though Alison when very young was found in her net one morning playing happily with one of these hideous creatures!

Though it had bitten her, it was thankfully not infected so didn't infect her. And Elizabeth's blood test following a possible bite one time was also negative. A bite can be fatal, though more often than not the victim can live a good long life afterwards, as in the case of Bishop David who had been bitten when young.

One afternoon we prepared for the anti-chagas brigade by moving furniture away from walls and putting foodstuffs in the car ready for their 7:15am arrival next day, by which time we were sitting outside by a blazing fire. Once their task was done we set about cleaning.

Another year things didn't go quite so smoothly. The man arrived at 9am, three hours after we'd got up to clear the kitchen, remove the mattresses and move the furniture. The poison used was *gammexane* and he was going round all the mission houses and other buildings, spraying with pink outside and white inside. He decided our house would be the last to be treated and by the time he got to us at 1pm he'd run out of white, so without consulting us splattered our nice white interior walls pink. When we entered after he'd gone, we knew not whether to laugh or cry. We decided on the former and thought of modern art. Some time later caretaker Emilio restored them to their traditional colour; and no *vinchuca* was seen there again.

Health and Safety? What's that?

The Argentine visitor who described our life in the Chaco as *"muy precario"* was not wrong, provided it was remembered, as stated earlier, that much more precarious was that of the people whose real home it is. Alison went down with hepatitis A soon after our return to Juárez in 1988 and Margaret had suffered a mysterious long-standing illness before we met. Then there were the near-accidents at a time before 'health and safety' was invented. On holiday in the Córdoba area we visited a park and Alison, still a toddler, slipped through a gap in a hedge and wandered on to the flat roof of a hut. She was right on the edge of a horrible fall when Margaret spotted her and raced to snatch her away.

Another disaster was avoided in Juárez when Elizabeth was seen clinging to the top of the empty *aljibe* of one of the mission houses. This was a tank to catch rainwater and her legs were dangling down the inside, but thankfully I managed to lift her up and out. She also had problems in a children's playground in Salta, falling from the near-top rung of the ladder of a slide, but once more we were grateful to God that she was just grazed and shaken.

Shortly after Alison started school, Margaret picked her up one lunchtime and they set off on the bicycle to visit our Norwegian Pentecostal missionary friends, Brígido and Britt. Crossing the railway at a point where they had to cycle down a slope, they found a wire at neck-height across their way. There was no time to react; Alison was thrown off and Margaret was left with a sore neck and bruises on her upper arms.

There was Wimbledon – or rather, Embarcación. One day in the Mission there the girls, having watched some other children playing tennis, decided to try it. They hadn't got a ball, but no problem because stretched across the compound was a wire with a heavy iron hook on it. Elizabeth 'served' by pushing the hook along and it just missed Alison's eye, cutting her face badly. Our missionary colleague Dr Hugo Vergara attended to her at the hospital, though she wouldn't let him stitch the wound. The evidence is still there today if you look ever so closely.

Our neighbour Chris decided to set up beehives in the Mission at Juárez, and one day when he collected the honey four of them came over and stung me as I sat outside. Another time I was trapped in my office in the garden, unable to return to the house as the creatures buzzed around. Indeed, the launch of the Wichi New Testament in Misión Chaqueña in 1992 had a sting in the tail when a boy released a swarm of bees across the Mission in revenge for not being entitled to a share of the communal stewpot. Fortunately, the ceremony had been completed but the bees ensured folk stayed indoors for an hour or two afterwards.

25
More wildlife

Bees were the least of our concerns. One Sunday morning on arriving back from church we found our garden had been a battlefield with flying ants trying to take over the nests of their earthbound cousins. The latter won and the place was full of winged corpses. I spent the afternoon cleaning out the rear guttering, removing scores of dead flyers. But two months later another battle ensued as flying ants swept in to lay their eggs. I waded in with *gammexane* and soon waded out, stung all over as the beasts got into jeans, socks and shoes, before a builder came to the rescue.

One day we killed a huge spider hiding behind the girls' toy bricks in the patio and on another I terminated a tarantula which had been in their paddling-pool. Then a very poisonous snake, a *yarará*, a species that attacks, emerged from a hole in the patio and an indian lad killed it. I killed a baby of the same venomous type in their bedroom, and one day two frontier policemen spotted a large one slithering across the road towards the Mission. It escaped into a hole which one of them fired shots into, but the beast slipped out the other end, mouth open and leaping at the other. Thankfully they managed to kill it with a spade.

The expert in snake lore lived in Misión La Paz. Artín would catch *yararás* and other poisonous species and put them, still alive, in a tin for dispatch to Buenos Aires for serum. This genial backwoodsman would never see such a cosmopolitan city but his work perhaps saved many lives.

Snakes, spiders, and of course scorpions. Jesus' followers have authority to trample on scorpions, according to Luke's Gospel, and Margaret was literally unharmed one night when she trod on one when walking barefoot by torchlight in the girls' bedroom.

Ticks can be painful when the head stays buried under the skin, and this happened to Margaret when she tried to remove such a beast that had burrowed into her. It came at a time when our salary was delayed in arriving from Salta and she had to buy groceries on tick. My pun was not appreciated.

One day a Wichi pastor arrived from the River Pilcomayo area with an unhealed piranha bite on his ankle. He'd walked half a day from the river back to his home, losing a lot of blood on the way, and had cadged a lift to Juárez for hospital treatment. Many were the fishermen who suffered in this way; indeed, it was a kind of badge of honour to be so bitten.

Domestics

It wasn't just the wildlife that brought trouble. Margaret and the girls are dog lovers (I'm keeping quiet) and when we returned to Argentina in 1984 after the Falklands hiatus, Alison and Elizabeth wanted one as a pet. It seemed a good idea to help them through the enormous change of culture from historic Durham to hysterical Juárez. So we got Paddy - for a while. This puppy soon grew into a sizeable bounder, and despite spending a night locked in church and regularly accompanying our nurse colleague Helen Sohns to hospital alongside her motor cycle, he showed little sanctification or compassion, instead becoming the town terror. One day he injured a she-goat belonging to an elderly lady, and when Margaret went to see her he followed and nearly killed a pig. The lady reckoned the goat's unborn kid died as a result of the attack and then the goat too died.

Paddy chased pigs and hens and once we arrived home to find a local rancher announcing that our dog had killed one of his she-goats. He wanted to charge us a huge amount, but we paid him half after two butchers independently valued a she-goat at roughly that. But it was the end for Paddy. A lady we knew took him to her brother's ranch about 50 kilometres away, where he died of illness not long afterwards.

We had other dogs and a very fertile cat, given to us as male but proving otherwise. Our last dog, Tsuku, arrived as a stray covered in ticks and fleas. "You've come to a good home", Helen said to him as Margaret bathed him and I walked the other way in search of a job that couldn't wait. Tsuku never got to church like Paddy, but he did go to school with Elizabeth one day and sat under her desk all morning. He died in our last year there after a struggle to recover from a fight with another dog.

Margaret's pet armadillo

For dealing with ants!

26
Learning to communicate (with difficulty)

Sometimes people ask me how I started to learn Wichi and how long it took.

The answer to the second is that I never stopped learning, new discoveries arising almost daily. As to the start I was, as mentioned earlier, well tutored by Bishop Patrick Harris, an excellent speaker of the language. I was then let loose to spend time with the people, to listen and practise, and over time built up a good knowledge of vocabulary and grammar, though it wasn't until I met Francisco Pérez in Misión La Paz that I made great strides forward in understanding, linguistic analysis and speaking.

Some of the early days in Misión Chaqueña gave me memorable conversations about the language, though not always for the right reasons. One day I was wondering about the conjugation of the word *oläy*, which means 'I'm alive' and 'I'm full up' (after eating). Old Andrés happened to appear at my open mosquito-netted window and peered in, not an unusual occurrence for an indian, and so I decided to enter into negotiations:

"Andrés, tell me, the Wichi for *estoy repleto* (= 'I'm full up' in Spanish), is *oläy*, isn't it?"

"Sí, *oläy*. If I eat a lot, *oläy.*"

"Now suppose you're full, how do you say that?"

"*Oläy.*"

"No, I mean, suppose I want to say, 'You're full', what do I say to you?"

"Sí, *oläy.*"

"Sorry, no, Andrés. Let's try again. What is the Wichi for 'you are full'?"

"Well, if I've eaten a lot, *oläy.*"

I was beginning to wish I'd never started this. One more try:

"Andrés, how do you say, 'he is full'?"

"*Iläy.*"

"Right, now how do you say, 'you are full'? Or, to make it clearer, suppose I want to ask you, 'Are you full, Andrés', what would I say to you?"

"Sí, *oläy.* I've had a big dinner."

"No, that's what you'd say to me. What would I say to you? Would I say, *Ha aläy?* or *Ha leläy?*"

"Well, if two of us sat down to eat, when we'd finished, I'd say of him that *iläy* and of me that *oläy.*"

"*Ha aläy?* or *Ha leläy?*"

"Yes."

Communicating (with difficulty)

These are days of instant communication. I've just checked a couple of facts on the internet and regularly participate via Zoom with Argentine folk in their living-rooms and offices over there during meetings on behalf of the companion link between the dioceses of Sheffield, in which we now live, and (South) Argentina. And when I visited the Chaco a few years ago, many of the indians had mobile phones and communication had become much easier and faster.

Not so long ago it was very different. The easiest way to send a message was to go yourself or send it, verbally or written, with a reliable person who happened to be going where your message needed to go. Across the diocese we had short-wave radio contact between certain centres three times a day. Communication had to be in Spanish and care was needed, especially when reception was poor. Once Margaret ordered tablets from Salta and the radio operator there came back next day to check if they were to benefit her health or kill rats; in Spanish her medicine was only one letter away from rat poison. I spent an age one afternoon trying to fathom why a pipe-smoking anthropologist friend was needing work. Reception problems meant I kept hearing *trabajo* (work) rather than *tabaco* (tobacco), which unknown to me he'd ordered via a colleague. But the radio, time-consuming though it was, acted as a lifeline – and a bearer of bad

110

tidings. News of family illnesses and deaths reached us by radio, having gone through various channels before they got to our remote home. If the bishop called you to the radio, it might mean a message of this kind and I had my unpleasant share of them. On the other hand it might be something altogether more encouraging, such as the publication of a portion of Bible translation that we'd worked hard on. Letters invariably followed and the postal service, local and international, though not speedy, was usually reliable.

You can't get full-time telephones

In Juárez we also had a telephone, 'we' meaning the town. This phone was staffed part-time and worked part-time; I reckon you could rely on it 30% of the time. Once I spent a frustrating period chasing up a mysterious message from Mennonite translators Albert and Lois Buckwalter in their distant home in the city of Roque Sáenz Peña, asking me to phone them. I assumed it was about an imminent visit from a Translations Consultant from the USA, Roger Omanson, so I waited for the next bus but he failed to appear on it. I then booked a phone call to the Buckwalters and waited in a queue at the small mud-brick building which was the exchange. Time passed so I slipped out to meet the next bus, but he wasn't on that either. And it was during my absence that the operator finally got through for me, so that when I returned to the exchange a man in the queue greeted me pitilessly with the words, *"Perdiste el turno"* (You've missed your turn"). I gave up and returned next morning at 8, finally getting through to learn the real travel details. (The saga of Roger's delayed journey is told in Part 2 of this memoir.)

We always know here when the clocks go forwards or backwards, but over there it was not necessarily so. One morning at 8am I got a shock when Isidro turned up for a translation session and told me it was 9am. He'd heard it on the radio: someone had decided the clocks should go forward for summer.

Radio and telephone somehow combined to inform me one time of a week-long computer workshop at the Paraguayan Bible Society in

Asunción. So I travelled overnight by two buses and arrived at the home of Bishop John Ellison and his wife Judie early on Sunday morning. Judie greeted me warmly but with surprise, not knowing I was coming. Apparently our Northern Argentina Diocesan Office in Salta had phoned that I was coming but the line was poor. Bishop John was a great supporter of Chaco ministry, and unabashed at my sudden epiphany whipped me off after breakfast to a service at which he interviewed me and invited me to assist at Communion. The course began next day and the coordinator also expressed surprise when I appeared: apparently someone had told her I couldn't come because of a meeting back in Argentina. I began to feel like the unheralded one – but with the communications we had in those days, such things were unsurprising!

Find my ring!

One evening a woman unknown to me arrived on our doorstep sent by her relative, a friend of ours. She wanted help in locating her ring, lost three years ago 50 kilometres away in Chiriguanos. I was bewildered. Did she want me to pray? To contact the church leaders there? "No, I've heard you've got a computer. Consult that!" She claimed to have seen one in Buenos Aires which located missing objects!

I was the first person in Juárez to have a computer, provided by the United Bible Societies for the translation project. It made an enormous difference, not least in time-saving, as corrections could be immediately inserted electronically into the drafts instead of these having to be retyped endless times on a typewriter. I could never have imagined how computing would grow and that communication would become as *instantáneo* as the milk we made our children from tins of powder in those days. I'm not sure, though, that computers can even now locate missing rings. Nor am I sure which I prefer: instant access to anyone and any fact, or the privacy and unconnectedness which allowed us to get on with life, family, people, and work. I think it's the latter.

27
"What do you do in the evenings?"

Some years after we returned to the UK, Margaret, now ordained and a Team Vicar in Essex, asked the congregation to name significant years in history. 1066 and 1914 came up, but she was puzzled when someone shouted "1989". It wasn't the Essex accent that flummoxed her; it was why that particular year was a momentous one. She asked the person to elucidate. "The Fall of the Berlin Wall", he said, wondering why she needed to be reminded of something so world-transforming.

When we lived in Juárez our world was a small place and we depended on the BBC World Service to remind us that there was a bigger one out there. I do recall hearing about the Fall of the Wall, and it was obviously an event of great moment and a cause for jubilation, but in terms of life in the Chaco it took place over the hills and far away on some distant continent. We were like the Sunday School children in Juárez who were asked to name a country. Apart from Argentina, they could only come up with Paraguay, Brazil, England and the USA.

The World Service was one of the answers to the question "What do you do in the evenings?" posed by a visitor from the UK who'd noted the lack of a television – in fact, the lack of electricity in that location. Another answer was Scrabble. Meals shared with colleagues, local folk and visitors were also what we often 'did in the evenings', and we sometimes went to one of the four weekly meetings at the Centre Church.

Outside broadcast
Then cable television came to Juárez. We resisted it for a while until one cold winter's afternoon we found Alison and Elizabeth standing outside a friend's house near the Mission peering at TV through the window. So we had it installed and for the last year of our sojourn our

children had the pleasure of watching Argentina's output, which in those days was hardly edifying but kept them entertained.

Entertain yourselves

One evening Margaret took Alison and our neighbours' boys, Juan Francisco and Camilo, to a film about Jesus at the school. It was in black and white, ancient and scratched, the dialogue was inaudible, and the projector broke down every few minutes and had to be dismantled, fixed and reassembled. Eventually Margaret took the children and walked out, demanding her 90 cents back and getting it.

She went with Juan and Camilo's mother, Ana, and our combined total of six children to another film show in the school, but this time it was those in charge who went out and failed to return. Another time Alison and Elizabeth attended a party in the Roman Catholic Church Hall. The room was dirty and the comfortable chairs, springs protruding, could have come out of the ark. After the protracted tea, consisting of an unidentifiable drink and an endless supply of biscuits, there was disorganisation until two clowns, dressed more like pirates, appeared to entertain the young guests. With all this, small wonder that on arrival in the UK for leave in 1987 our girls were described good-naturedly by a former missionary as *"muy formoseñas"* – very much children of the remote eastern Chaco, and by another friend as "not UK street-wise". They adapted rapidly, as children do.

Margaret and I have always been avid readers. In the Chaco we read anything available, usually in English, and shared books and magazines around with colleagues. When the weekly *Manchester Evening News Football Pink* turned up in the post (not necessarily a weekly occurrence), I looked forward to the next siesta or free evening to catch up on sport in the UK. One day Margaret packed a box of old books in English to send by truck to colleagues over the border in Asunción, Paraguay. Unfortunately it became confused with a box of newly-arrived Bibles, which was mistakenly loaded on to the truck instead. Thankfully, the error was spotted just before departure; otherwise, Margaret's accompanying note, "We've read all these and

114

have finished with them", could have caused some embarrassment!

It didn't really matter what we did in the evenings, because life in general was entertaining, not least for its surprises and unpredictabilities. One Wichi backwoodsman, a regular visitor, always gave us cause to smile, such as the time he arrived to return six unsold hymnbooks wrapped in a flour-bag and whitened by the experience. We chatted over bread and coffee, whose crumbs and dregs he then unceremoniously tipped over the floor! Fortunately carpets hadn't been invented there then.

I went to the Electricity Board to query why our two-monthly bill had gone up sixfold. I discovered that as well as costs rising, the more you used the higher the cost per unit! Still, it was only about £25 for three houses and the large garage.

An affair of the heart

There were the inevitable cross-cultural linguistic confusions. A *criolla* lady from Salta came to lead a course for Wichi and Toba Sunday School teachers. The sessions had to be in Spanish and the lady frequently used the word *corazón* ('heart'). Margaret pointed out that this was unhelpful as the heart's significance is different for the indians, an explanation which puzzled both the teacher and a Norwegian missionary who likewise didn't know either of the indian languages. So the latter asked a Wichi man if they had a word for 'heart' and then triumphantly announced to Margaret that yes, they had – it was *ot'otle*.

But that wasn't the point! They have a word for it, but its meaning is limited to the organ in the body and has nothing to do with emotions as it does in Spanish and English. For that they use *ohusek* or *ochowej*, the words for one's inner being.

28
A UK aftermath

Nothing can take away from us the joy and privilege of serving God and those of his people living in Northern Argentina. So when we returned to the UK in August 1991 we had the precious memories recaptured in this book. But there were more adventures ahead, though of different type and degree.

Margaret had wondered what the future held for her. Out of touch with recent developments in medicine, but much involved in church life, she suddenly said to me in bed early one morning in Juárez, "I just heard a voice say to me, 'Go to Cranmer Hall'". This is the theological college in Durham, the city that would be our base when we returned to the UK. Margaret's sister and brother-in-law had again kindly offered us accommodation in the flat on the end of their large house and Alison (11) and Elizabeth (9) were registered for local comprehensive and primary schools respectively. In addition, we had met the Principal of Cranmer Hall during our previous period of leave.

I was much encouraged by this voice and urged Margaret to follow it up. She did and in October 1991 began a three-year course of study there, one of her colleagues being a certain Justin Welby, who went on to become Bishop of Durham and then Archbishop of Canterbury. Margaret didn't quite reach those heights but served in two Essex parishes, St Margaret's Stanford-le-Hope, where she did her curacy under Rev. John Guest, and St Michael's Rayleigh, where she became Team Vicar under Rev. David Parrott. Those were generally happy years, and our daughters adapted well to Essex ways and words and went on to university at Bradford and Nottingham (my old stamping-ground) respectively.

Mission in South Yorkshire
The time came for Margaret to seek her final stipendiary post, and after

looking at a number of parishes she phoned Rev. David Bent, Rector of the Rivers Team of four churches in South Yorkshire. Months earlier he had contacted her about the vacancy at one of those churches, St Lawrence Tinsley in Sheffield, but she was looking elsewhere at the time. However, she kept it in mind and her call led to a visit to the area during which she rang me to say, "I've found a parish I'd really like to work in". She was accepted and in July 2003, days before Elizabeth graduated from Nottingham University, we upped sticks, left Essex and returned north. For Margaret, who hails from Sheffield, it was near to a homecoming, and she went on to serve at Tinsley for over seven years, up to and beyond retirement.

It took me longer to adapt to Tinsley than to anywhere else I'd lived – including Juárez! Even now when I drive through the town, the chorus of that Benny Hill mock-protest song from the 1960s starts to go through my head: "What a world! What a place! Ain't yer glad yer a member of the human race?"

But Tinsley grew on me, with its friendly people and mission opportunities. Its multi-ethnic population includes a large Asian element and a smaller Eastern European one, but it was to refugees and asylum seekers that Margaret found herself drawn in ministry as folk from Iran and parts of Africa landed on our doorstep and the church's, having been housed in the parish by local government. She calculates there were 39 of these, some of whom became good friends, including the one who commented that there can be only 500 women in the world like Margaret. Together with serving the predominantly white church members, she was in her element as the challenges and demands of cross-cultural ministry years before in Argentina re-emerged in a South Yorkshire working-class town.

29
A UK-Argentina aftermath

But for me, before Tinsley, and during Durham and Essex, there was … Argentina. During our final year there as a family, a group of Wichi pastors and church leaders sat in our living-room one morning and discussed the Bible. "You've got a complete one in English", one said. Nods all round. "The *criollos* have got a complete one, and now they've got a new translation of it." More energetic nodding. "So when you've finished translating the New Testament into our words, what are you going to do about the Old?" Nodding turns to prodding.

I'd wondered about this myself, not least because Bill Mitchell, our former Translations Consultant from the United Bible Societies (UBS), had himself done Old Testament translation in Peru and left me intrigued about the prospect. Though we would soon be returning as family to the UK, support was not lacking for the challenge of forming a Wichi team of translators in Argentina, coordinated by myself in the UK, where I would work on their drafts and then spend up to three months of each year over there with them. Bishop David Leake and his successor Maurice Sinclair both heartily supported the project, as did the Diocese of Northern Argentina, the Wichi leaders themselves, the Argentine Bible Society, the United Bible Societies, the South American Mission Society – and not least Margaret and the family, despite the separations it would entail.

The wonder that it all happened
The story of the Old Testament in Wichi, with its ups and downs, is told in Part 2 of this memoir. As I look back now, I marvel at how it all happened: all those typewritten drafts posted in Argentina and reaching me in Durham or Essex to work through; those painful twice-yearly goodbyes; those flights across the Atlantic and day-long bus journeys through Argentina; those cultural readjustments to basic living conditions; those six-day working weeks, plus preaching at least

once on Sundays; those perilous endings to times there. In regard to these I twice found myself stuck in Juárez due to unseasonal rain and buses not turning up. Each time God stooped to rescue me by the provision of a diocesan pick-up truck and a competent Wichi driver and helpers to get me through the long muddy distance to tarmac roads and, eventually, a plane home. Once I'd reached Buenos Aires, 1000 miles from Juárez, I was always wonderfully well looked after by Bishop David Leake (who was by now Bishop of Argentina, the other Anglican diocese in that vast country) and his wife Rachel. Then there was Pepe, a faithful taxi driver who got me to and from the airport in a vehicle sometimes minus the glass in one of its windows. Whenever we drove past a church he would cross himself, and I expressed my gratitude to God silently for His care and provision.

In Juárez I often stayed on the end of the Mission garage in a two-roomed flat for visitors which I always booked under the ironic name 'The Garden Mews'. It was basic but comfortable and was both living accommodation and study where the translators and myself worked. I was well supported by missionaries Peter and Rev. Sue Murray, Michael and Silvia Browne and René and Marina Pereira who occupied the houses on the Mission. The one translator who didn't live in Juárez or its wider area was Yolanda Alfaro, and so most work with her was conducted in her village of Misión Chaqueña where my Argentine sojourn had begun back in 1977. One of the six launches of the Wichi Bible in 2002 was held there, and a week later it was a joy to have Juan Toribio, Yolanda and Isidro at the most prestigious and memorable of them, held in the Teatro Avenida (theatre) in Buenos Aires.

Superlink

How did I feel after all those years? Elated. Relieved. Weary. But always privileged and grateful to God to have served him and the particular people of his called the Wichi. Thankful, too, for churches that had upheld the work over the years in prayer and financial support. At one point we had 18 of these 'link churches', as they were called, and it was a proud day in 2003 when I was able to visit St Mary, Hawkshaw, in Lancashire and present them with a copy of the Wichi Bible. St Mary was more than a link: I called it a 'superlink' because of the friendship that developed over nearly 25 years, nurtured by regular correspondence from the excellent Missionary Secretary, Betty Hodgson, and the wonderfully supportive vicar, Rev. Eric Ruehorn, and his wife Vera. This was an example of true partnership in a project between a UK church and an overseas people-group, facilitated by a mission agency.

'Superlink' congregation of Hawkshaw send greetings to Argentina

30
A new resource

In the latter days of the Wichi translation project, during proofreading and the subsequent wait for publication and launch, I was sometimes asked to help in small tasks at the SAMS office in Selly Oak, Birmingham. Then the Communications Secretary, an ex-missionary in Chile, was invited to return to her former job there as head of a Christian school, so I was asked to cover for her for three months … then six … and finally, keep going! The job title was changed to Resources Officer and I reckon I got the job, with its rather grand title, because my knowledge and experience of SAMS over the years was a useful resource to start with. But I had a real sense of God's hand on the whole business.

So my travels began again, but instead of planes it was car and trains as I travelled to Birmingham, first from Essex, then from Sheffield. Next door to my office was that of Bishop David Evans, General Secretary of the Society, who occupied the domestic part of the property with his wife Dorothy. They had been missionaries in Argentina before David was consecrated as Bishop of Peru and Bolivia. Years later he invited me to provide editorial assistance for his two books, *Have stick, will travel* and *40 years in purple*.

A new PA
Pattie Dixie, another ex-missionary colleague in Argentina, eased me into the job and was a wonderful PA in the early days. When she moved on, her replacement was close to home – very close, in fact, in the shape of my daughter Elizabeth. Some time before, I'd been invited to preach at the church in Treeton, Rotherham, the former pit village to which we've since retired. I was by now a Licensed Reader in the Church of England, and on this particular Sunday as I entered the church I picked up the latest newsletter of the Diocese of Sheffield and noticed on the back a small advertisement for a part-time Assistant

Secretary to the Bishop of Sheffield. I told Elizabeth, who applied and got the job. Some time later she found herself occupying the other half of her time as my PA at SAMS! We travelled together each week to Birmingham, until an office was rented for us in a parish centre in Sheffield.

The SAMS library and archive was transferred from Birmingham to an adjacent room in Sheffield and proved an invaluable resource in the work. It contained some priceless items, the most precious of all being the final diary of Captain Allen Gardiner, R.N., the naval officer who founded the Society in 1844 and perished from starvation, with his six colleagues, in an attempt to reach the Yahgan people at Argentina's wild southern tip in 1851. The diary was discovered the following year on the shore next to his body, in remarkably good condition despite the elements, and including his final entry from the day of his death – a struggling pencil yet revealing a faithful and contented soul. His life and death proved a catalyst for the ministry of SAMS over the next 150 years and beyond.

For seven years Elizabeth and I produced the quarterly SAMS magazine, *Share*, and Prayer Diary together with other printed resources to support the work in South America and also in Spain and Portugal, the Anglican work in these countries having come under SAMS' auspices some years before. We also developed the online presence through a new website, in partnership with graphic designer John Morse-Brown in Birmingham. But the challenges facing the Society were becoming too great and a merger with the larger Church Mission Society (CMS) was effected in 2010. This was a painful time for us all; nevertheless, CMS has welcomed all connected with SAMS, and at the same time the special SAMS ethos and 'family spirit' have been kept alive by the Latin Forum which has organised special annual events for the 'SAMS family' under the heading *Adelante!* 'Onward!'

Although Elizabeth and I both lost our jobs, she was given extra responsibilities by the Bishop of Sheffield until she was appointed Executive Assistant at Church House, the headquarters of the Diocese of Sheffield. I retired, but find myself as chairman and a Latin America representative of a regional CMS committee as well as a member of the working group which handles the Sheffield side of the longstanding companion link between the dioceses of Argentina and Sheffield. I write once or twice a year for the daily Bible reading devotional, *Living Light,* and volunteered at the CLC Christian bookshop in Sheffield for ten years until its sad closure early in 2021. I am also asked from time to time to read through and check drafts of new publications in Wichi. Margaret and I worship in the Rotherham parishes of Wales, Harthill and Thorpe Salvin, a few miles from Treeton. We're grateful to God to be still active in ministry, especially in leading worship and preaching.

"Make it a Wichi Bible study"

I enjoy public speaking – perhaps more than one-to-one conversation! Sometimes I'm presented with a challenge to be grappled with. One morning, soon after my appointment as Resources Officer of SAMS, Bishop David Evans popped into my office in Birmingham and with characteristic directness said, "Bob, it's SAMS General Council in a fortnight; I'd like you to do the Bible study." "Right ... yes ... David ... fine", I replied with hesitant acquiescence.

He left as abruptly as he'd entered, but then popped his head round my door and said, "Make it a Wichi Bible study".

A Wichi Bible study? What on earth did he mean? I was momentarily nonplussed and still don't know what he might have had in mind. I laughed to myself at the thought of doing a Bible study in that language and leaving the General Council not understanding a word. But immediately a seed-thought came to me, an idea I'd vaguely mulled over before. How about introducing the listeners to a session of Bible translation, like so many I'd done with my colourful translator colleague, Isidro Vilte, over the years? I would need to do a bit of play-acting, playing both Isidro and myself as we wrestled with a passage of Scripture to render it accurately and sensitively across languages and cultures into the Wichi tongue. It would also demonstrate the challenge of cooperation between two people of very different cultures

123

– and personalities – together handling the Word of God.

So it came to pass. I chose the Beatitudes because that passage contains many of the issues we'd discussed and even argued over. I prepared it with enthusiastic thoroughness, delivered it at General Council (perhaps enjoying the play-acting too much) and found it to be warmly received. It helped that several people knew Isidro and were familiar with his idiosyncracies. But one who didn't said she'd learned more about Bible translation in those 20 minutes (I'm sure it was 30) than ever before.

I've used the Wichi Bible Study in churches and conferences over the years. Sometimes it comes off well, sometimes it produces little reaction: there's a time for everything under heaven, even a Wichi Bible Study. My friend and former SAMS colleague Richard Crofts has used it, or parts of it, in meetings he's led, giving it doubtless his own particular touch. You can read the original version in Appendix 2 to Part 2 of this memoir.

APPENDIX

The Travails of a Gendarme

This story was recounted to me by a Gendarme, a frontier policeman from Buenos Aires deployed to serve in Juárez, 1,000 miles from home, in the 1980s. It was the wee small hours of a Sabbath day as we sat outside Juárez station in a National Frontier Police jeep listening to the persistent rain on the tarpaulin roof. This man and his driver colleague had picked me up a couple of hours before as I made my way home from Saturday night church service – it's not a crime, they were simply sympathetic to my attempts to keep feet on the Juárez main road slime. And when they heard that I had to go out later to the station to meet a visitor possibly coming on the *ferrobús* railcar from Formosa, they readily offered to give me another lift as they too were expecting a colleague on it.

So here we were in the station 'car-park'. We'd been told roughly how late the train would be, had persuaded the local café owner to stay open a few minutes longer so we could drink a Coca-Cola, watched the jeep driver wade into the 'car-park' ditch to test the water level, driven across it, and were now whiling away the hours in the jeep: a Gendarme from Buenos Aires, another from elsewhere in Argentina, and a missionary from England … Cheshire … Winsford – as they'd asked, meaninglessly, to know. Here we were, gazing upon Juárez's latest collection of goods wagons – a time for the man from the national capital to reminisce, and to reveal that you didn't have to come from overseas to experience homesickness and culture shock.

"No", he said. "I got homesick even before I got to Juárez." In Formosa, in fact. I thought, 'If this is the provincial capital, what on earth can the interior be like?' I was fresh up from Buenos Aires and the Formosa folk put me up in a room with private bathroom, all so tiny you could do everything taking one stride in any direction. Yes, literally everything. Then I had to decide how to get to Juárez. They said it was ten or twelve hours' journey by either bus or *'ferrobús'*. *'Ferrobús'*, I pondered. 'That sounds an attractive name for a train. It must be modern, European, fully air-conditioned. I'll make for that.'

"'*Ferrobús* – modern?' someone said on hearing my thoughts. 'You must be joking. It's a *batata*. [Literal translation: sweet potato; idiomatic translation: shambles.]

"So I started to have second thoughts. Anyway, they'd told me there were a lot of snakes in the interior, and the *ferrobús* didn't get in till midnight while the bus arrived in Juárez at 5pm, in daylight. Yes, that sounded a better idea. At least in daylight I'd have less chance of stepping on such a beast. So off I trotted to the bus-station, bought my ticket, and early next morning I was on my way to Juárez.

"Fighting my homesickness, I dozed off to sleep. When I awoke, two things drew my attention away from the all-encircling forest. First, we were no longer on tarmac. The surface was just earth. This mainline highway, along which long-distance coaches like this one travelled daily, was apparently a dirt road. Very interesting. Second, it was lightning all around. Having observed these phenomena, I fell asleep once more.

"When I woke again, this time with a start, my view of the world had changed. Pouring rain from total cloud cover was now uppermost, the bus and I were in a ditch, and the passengers were scrambling at crazy angles to the top of the roadside. My first journey into the interior in a mainline coach had come to an untidy end and my homesickness deepened.

"Soon a road-levelling machine turned up and offered to take on any passenger who wanted to travel. I volunteered – the only one. Perhaps the others knew something I didn't. Anyway I boarded and clung upright to a stanchion for the less-than-breakneck-speed journey which got me as far as Lomitas. There I popped into a hotel, removed my sodden clothes, and fulfilling the instructions drummed into me in Buenos Aires put on white shirt, jacket and tie and reported to the local Frontier Police headquarters. They looked at me as if I'd arrived from Mars. 'What on earth are you dressed like that for? Up here we wear tee-shirt and jeans. This isn't Buenos Aires, you know.'

"I'd worked that out already. After giving me a bed for a while, they took me in a Ford Falcon to the station – to catch the *ferrobús*. I marched up to a man and asked for a ticket to Juárez. He too looked upon me as an interplanetary visitor. He then illuminated two things for me: one, he was the sweets salesman; two, tickets are purchased on the train. So I proceeded to wait with the other passengers... and wait.

"Eventually someone spotted the train's light illuminating the forest night. I saw it as the signal to gather my bags and move to the platform edge. I soon realised that no one else interpreted it that way and that my action had attracted considerable interest among my would-be fellow travellers. What I discovered was that this railway line is so straight and the forest around so dark that you can see the light of an approaching train a good 20 minutes before it actually reaches the station.

"But finally it arrived and we boarded. Well, you've never seen anything like it. It was standing room only, with 'room' a questionable element. I'd assumed the *ferrobús* was a train of normal length rather than just a bus on rails. At least it was air-conditioned – the windows opened. I spent the journey leaning forward at a precarious angle clinging to a luggage rack in front of a window, and when we stopped at a station I was almost strangled by hands reaching all around me to grab sandwiches 'freshly' made on the spot by an unshaven salesman on the platform edge. 'Sandwich, señor?' he enquired amidst the jousting and jostling. 'Er ... no thanks. I had a Coca-Cola in Lomitas', I replied.

"We set off again into the darkness until an emergency application of the brakes precipitated a chain of collapsed scrummages along the carriage. Some of us got out to discover a cow expired on the track. 'Beef sandwiches on the return journey', someone remarked with ominous seriousness as we heaved it to the side. At least the train was not damaged. Gon-gon-gon-gon.

Or so we thought. Gon-gon-gon. It's not starting again. Gon-gon ... fzzzzz. The driver emerged to issue a request. Would four gentlemen please get out and give him a push to try to get this thing started? I descended into the darkness, looking warily and treading likewise for the supposedly ubiquitous poisonous snakes of the area, all the time my mind boggling at the thought of explaining to my family in a letter that I'd spent my first night in the interior pushing a train. I know what they'd think. They'd picture the long swish trains of the capital, attempt to conjure up sights of folk push-starting them, and …. some things are unimaginable.

"Mind you, since I've been in Juárez I've had an experience even more bizarre. I bet you've never push-started a plane. I have. One day down at the airstrip a plane from Formosa wouldn't start and as I and a few others happened to be down there, they asked us to give it a push. Yes, I'm quite serious.

"We failed in our attempt to start the train, and so the driver issued another communiqué. They'd have to send for a mechanic. Where from? someone asked. Formosa. In the meantime, to preserve the battery he'd have to put the lights out. Good-night.

"Standing in an overloaded, blacked-out train in the middle of the night in the middle of nowhere is not a desirable experience, and so most of us stepped out and lay on the ground. I wondered what tomorrow would bring. It brought a pick-up truck and a lorry, both empty and heading for Juárez, so most of us hopped on, the final stage of my first adventure into the interior.

"Then after an initial interview here at which I was told that our chief role was to help the townsfolk, I was left to wander around aimlessly for days. But one day the commandant called me in. 'I've got a very important job for you, boy.' 'Yes, sir.' 'I want you to go and round up some pigs'.

"All my life flashed before me, especially my years of education and training. Now I knew what it was for. To come here to push trains and round up pigs. Juárez. Juárez. Come on, let's get out. The train could be here any hour."

PART 2

Wichi Bible Translation 1981-2002

1
The rise and fall of Black Cover

The first translation of the New Testament into the Wichi language was published in 1962. Translated by long-serving missionary Henry Grubb with substantial assistance from Alberto González, later one of the first ordained Wichi pastors, as well as certain other Wichi Christians, notably Martín Chilango, it was known as *P'ot Chalaj*, 'Black Cover', and much loved and used. It benefitted from portions of the New Testament translated down the years, beginning with Mark's Gospel, the work of pioneer missionary Richard Hunt and published by the British and Foreign Bible Society in 1919, the first publication in Wichi.

The 1962 translation was based, as all previous portions, on the dialect of the area of Misión Chaqueña where the Anglican mission had first been established (although neither González nor Chilango was from there). The base text used by Grubb was the English Revised Version (1885), described by one commentator as "that most acute of English versions" for its sturdy literalness. Nevertheless, wrote Grubb, "our aim was ... an idiomatic text, which the people would have no difficulty in following, even though there was no missionary at hand to help them" (*Chaco Jubilee* [unpublished report] 1962?). *P'ot Chalaj* proved helpful across the Chaco; however, it often strayed into literalness and some parts were difficult to understand, particularly in the epistles. The writer recalls a pastor reading a portion one day in church and then announcing that he had no idea what it meant. Probably a result of St Paul's thinking allied to a heavy literal rendering!

P'ot Chalaj was subsequently reprinted with a green paperback cover by the Sociedad Bíblica Argentina (SBA). However, by the 1970s there had emerged in both Spanish and English truly idiomatic and so-called 'functional equivalence' translations such as *Today's English Version* of the New Testament (subsequently part of the *Good News Bible)* and *Dios llega al hombre* (the title of the complete Bible was *Dios habla hoy).* Conscious of these developments into more accessible versions of Scripture, the SBA declined to consider any further reprint of *P'ot Chalaj*, opening the way for a new translation into Wichi using the principles of these 'functional equivalence' versions, which sought in the main to translate *sense* rather than aim at word-for-word exactness.

When the challenge of this new translation was addressed in the 1970s, it was felt appropriate to have a native speaker as translator, someone gifted in the depth and nuances of the language, and with a good theological understanding, while the missionary would serve alongside as theological, linguistic and literary adviser. The United Bible Societies (UBS), who oversaw the project and contributed to it in a financial and advisory way, referred to the adviser as the 'exegete'.

The formation of a translation pairing

I came from the UK in 1977 to coordinate this project, which necessitated an initial three-year study of the language in some of its dialects, mainly those of Misión Chaqueña and of the River Pilcomayo area with its regional variations, together with a less ample study of the Bermejo dialect, represented by folk who had migrated to the town of Ingeniero Juárez and its surroundings. After this period came the challenge of finding a Wichi person capable of undertaking the translation of the New Testament. Three gifted men were recommended to me by the then bishop, Patrick Harris: namely Francisco Pérez, Isidro Vilte and Juan Toribio.

Francisco had been my most able and enthusiastic language teacher who had helped me put many of the loose pieces of the Wichi linguistic jigsaw together; he was also a genial man and a friend. Isidro, on the other hand, appeared anything but genial; though clearly very able linguistically and theologically, he had strong opinions about everything and everyone and was dismissive of whatever irked him, including the idea of a new translation based, he wrongly assumed, on the dialect of Misión Chaqueña.

Juan I barely knew at the time. He had the advantage of being without work, whereas Francisco was an agricultural assistant and Isidro helped make programmes for Radio Amtena, the Wichi radio station. Yet Juan was something of a wanderer, never seemingly settled anywhere nor giving his mind to any one task for long – characteristics hardly suitable for a project that would take many years.

So Francisco's and Isidro's commitments ruled them out, as did Isidro's and Juan's characters, though Juan was later to play an immense part in the translation of the Old Testament. I considered a young man whom I'd taught at Bible School in 1979, and though he looked promising, as did his early trial drafts, I had reservations. Then one day I received, in my then home in Misión La Paz on the upper Pilcomayo, a message from him saying he didn't feel up to the task. It happened that same day that Isidro was visiting Misión La Paz from his home in Tartagal for a conference, and he handed me a piece of translation he'd done, seeking to improve some parts of an idiomatic version of Philippians made by Bishop Harris. This was a different Isidro from the one I'd known: he was approachable, his manner was pleasant and courteous. In addition the work he'd done was good, and all this set me wondering if God was pointing me in an Isidro direction, especially as his role at Radio Amtena was coming to an end, leaving him without work.

Soon afterwards, in March 1981, we had cause to visit Tartagal and I decided to grasp the nettle. I walked with my wife Margaret to Isidro's house in one of the Wichi neighbourhoods on the edge of town, but he was not at home. However, with the help of someone's directions in an area naturally without addresses, and with Margaret's determined persistence, we encountered him near the home of his wife's aunt. After brief pleasantries I asked him if he'd like to take on the work of New Testament translator. *"Okalhi"*, he replied – "I can". He added that he'd completed his corrections of Philippians and had also translated some Old Testament verses, probably some not included in the *Selecciones del Antiguo Testamento*, a slim book of parts of the Old Testament considered helpful to an understanding of the New and published by the SBA in 1971.

"So it may be", my diary records, "that the search for a translator of God's Word has ended in a shady track in a poor neighbourhood with a man on a bike near his wife's aunt's house looking for work."

He could indeed do the job, and the next 21 years were an adventure as New Testament was followed by Old and a respectful friendship developed. "We never had an argument", Isidro told someone when it was all done. Oh no?! If only! But he always felt there was a call upon his life and that God had kept him for this work. He told me more than once how as a baby on a journey with his family he appeared to have died and his father dug his grave, only for him to revive. As an adult he was dying in his home village of San Andrés until making a sudden and dramatic recovery.

It should be noted that all three suggested translators came from the River Pilcomayo area – Francisco from the upper reaches, Isidro and Juan from downstream. So the translation would focus on the northern way of speaking, appropriate because the language always seemed richer and more deeply rooted there and my most eager and knowledgeable informants hailed from those parts.

Author with Francisco, a great language helper

Isidro, a great translator, at work

Juan, another excellent translator

2
Promising beginnings

The work began with an hour in Tartagal in late April on the opening verses of Mark, the book chosen as the starter, being predominantly narrative, shorter than the other Gospels and not as theologically complex. We worked well together, and far from objecting, as I expected, he became excited when I suggested switching John the Baptist's preaching into direct speech. He and his wife and four youngest children arrived in La Paz in mid-May and he was immediately asking about the puzzle of Jesus' application of the quotation from Isaiah in Mark 4:12. A few days later he and Francisco met with me for a grammar session, Francisco trying to sort out one particular future imperative negative with a first person object – and with a disarming smile handing the problem over to Isidro! But perhaps life's too short for such matters!

One day Isidro flung his arms wide, rolled his head around and poured forth an emotion of words: "I sit up at night thinking about this new version. Then I go to bed still thinking about it. Then at 4am I wake up and I'm so excited by it all. It touches my heart because it's so clear. At times I want to cry." Another time he exclaimed "Alleluia!" after I'd read a portion of our work back to him. He was supposed to say "Good" or "Not clear enough" or "Needs improvement", but "Alleluia!" was a welcome reaction!

The translation process contained five stages:

1. Isidro drafted a translation of each passage. His base versions were the Spanish popular version, *Dios habla hoy* (DHH), and the standard literal version, the Reina Valera (RVR) in its 1960 revision. He also benefitted from a Roman Catholic translation entitled *El Libro del Pueblo de Dios* (The Book of God's People).

2. I checked his drafts using the Greek New Testament and various English versions, supported by the excellent *Translator's Handbooks* produced by the United Bible Societies and available for many books of the Bible. The Revised Standard Version was placed in the centre of my desk as first port of call to give me a fairly exact translation of the text in English.

3. We met together and worked carefully through the text.

4. At our next get-together I would read back to him what we'd agreed (and perhaps disagreed) upon and he would suggest improvements.

5. I would type up the agreed version.

When the New Testament was complete, we undertook a further thorough check, by which time our years of experience enabled us to make significant corrections and improvements.

Isidro was always careful to try to produce a version comprehensible to people in other areas, and when in the 1990s we came to the Old Testament he advised the other translators to seek to follow the same course. A Reading Committee of representatives from different areas was set up for the New Testament and they made suggestions for correcting and improving certain texts. It was the more controversial passages that were put before them.

Returning to the early days, the draft translation of Mark was completed after some time, followed by 1 John, and then we started Romans. Our decision to tackle this great and complex epistle so early perhaps betrayed a desire to try our skills and growing experience on a much more challenging book, a feeling that the Wichi needed its message – or over-confidence! It did lead, however, to a memorable 'awakening' two or three years later, after the hiatus of the Falklands War, when we were travelling along the River Pilcomayo visiting some of its villages and sleeping in the open. We were used to being awakened, still under starlit night, by barking dogs or crowing cocks. But that particular time it was a human voice that woke me, it was speaking Wichi and it was talking about a corpse. Furthermore, the speaker was announcing that he was the corpse, and he actually sounded pleased about it.

Whereupon the truth began to dawn upon me, even as the fleas in my sleeping-bag. Hadn't Isidro suggested we translate 'dead to sin' in Romans 6 as 'corpses in face of sin'? And didn't I read that portion in the villages we visited yesterday? And didn't he go to sleep wrapped in his blanket on the ground a few yards away from me? And don't the Wichi often pray aloud, especially first thing in the morning? And isn't Isidro prone to include bits of St Paul's theology in his prayers? So that was it!

Politics and war intervene, then promise renewed
When we'd reached the end of chapter 4 in March 1982, our time in Argentina came to a sudden end as the Falklands War broke out and drove several missionaries home to the UK, including ourselves. During the two years and five months that we were home, Isidro stuttered along with Romans, overseen from time to time by Australian missionary Stephen Barrett.

But in August 1984 we returned to Argentina and soon afterwards Isidro appeared on a brief visit to the city of Salta where we'd landed. We bowed to each other – evidently we'd learned one another's sense of humour – and then to my astonishment he said, "Is there any work we can do while I'm here?" So we found an office, sat down and resumed at Romans 5:1, looking back at the link with the end of Romans 4 that we'd translated back in 1982. It was if that 29-month hiatus had never happened.

With the restoration of democracy in the country we detected that people were able to breathe more easily, and there was also a freedom for indigenous rights groups to express themselves. The attitude to the use of indigenous languages was much more positive amongst both indians and *criollos*. Yet alongside a rediscovery of pride in the languages and cultures came disapproval by some Wichi parents of educational focus upon such things. Some were Christians who saw a clash between traditional Wichi customs and their faith, alongside the growing problems of alcoholism and immorality.

Juárez – translation hub

We went to live in Ingeniero Juárez (hereafter abbreviated to Juárez) in the Province of Formosa, and after a period of very slow progress Isidro and family moved there in 1985; the Wichi New Testament was once again full steam ahead. A supporter in the UK sent money to build him a house, which included an office where he worked on the translation day by day, often rising at 4am to do so. He lived there as ordained pastor, archdeacon – and retired translator – until his death at the age of 86 late in 2020 during my writing of these memoirs.

Slow progress in a session was always more satisfying as we felt we'd really wrestled with the text. Many verses covered in a session made us feel we might have missed something or taken some things for granted. Five verses of Ephesians 4 in two-and-a-half hours one day left us encouraged; even more so three verses of the Beatitudes in three hours, with particular focus on 'Blessed', 'poor in spirit' and 'meek'. See Appendix 2 on the Beatitudes.

There were many hiatuses, often caused by illness or problems within Isidro's family. And one day a white man stole his trousers while he slept outside; Isidro chased after him and fell in an unsuccessful attempt to arrest him, injuring himself in the process. With regard to his family, we sometimes felt that Satan was attacking the work by playing on this Achilles heel with their internal and external squabbles and dissensions.

On 22 March 1990 he finished drafting the New Testament, the last book we tackled and one of the most difficult being 2 Corinthians. He corrected a heretically faulty rendering of mine of 11:3 which implied that the people were in danger of wandering from their faithfulness to the serpent and turning to Christ. A few days later we began the final read-through, during which we found many shortcomings in our translations of Romans and 1 Corinthians; Romans chapter 3 proved especially challenging.

During our checking of Galatians, Isidro improved the challenging chapter 2 to such an extent that his work on this section was, to my mind, his finest of the New Testament. Especially noteworthy were the latter part of verse 5: *ot'amajej amhohen Dios Silätyaj tä häpe m'ak tä matche, wet nittäya tä i'amejen* ("we guarded for you God's Proclamation which is the truth, so that it never be not with you"), and the double use of the characteristic Wichi verb *w'enhayej* (meaning something like 'differented') in verse 9 to indicate the different ministries of the Jerusalem apostles and of Paul and Barnabas.

The read-through was completed in May 1991 and I subsequently read it through myself one final time, until I could say on 4 July, "It's done". Four floppy disks carried the entire New Testament. Three days later Isidro and I left on the long bus journey to Buenos Aires, via Formosa. There we handed them over to Ronald Hussey, then head of the Sociedad Bíblica Argentina, who later that week took them to the United Bible Societies in Miami to begin the process leading towards publication. His secretary reckoned he had the precious disks tied to his waist!

3
The Old follows the New

The New Testament was published by the SBA in a green hardback volume the following year. I was by this time living back in the UK for family reasons, but the project to translate the Old Testament was already underway. It had, as stated towards the end of Part 1 of this memoir, been requested by certain Wichi pastors and leaders, seeking parity with the *criollos* and Anglo-Saxon missionaries who "have the Word of God in their languages". The Diocese of Northern Argentina and the United Bible Societies were among those who agreed to the project and to its unusual *modus operandi* with the translators working in Argentina and myself in the UK.

Isidro was again chief translator but was supported throughout by Yolanda Alfaro from Misión Chaqueña and subsequently Juan Toribio and Ponciano Benítez, with some assistance from José Mariano Pérez, a relative of Ponciano and, like him, a state-employed nurse. I received their drafts through the post and worked on them in the UK, visiting Argentina for up to three months of each year, usually in two visits.

New translators for the Old
Yolanda's calling to the work was striking. Isidro and I visited her in 1991 in her home in Misión Chaqueña and asked her if she'd like to join the team of translators for the Old Testament project. She'd impressed us with her observations and comments as a member of the New Testament Reading Committee. Before I could finish putting the question to her, she answered yes and recounted two dreams that had puzzled her. In one she was told to pay attention to the *redactora* (editor), and in the other I appeared and told her she was to "feed my sheep" as we stood in front of a chart relating to malnutrition. Soon afterwards the indians' Rural Pastoral Committee voted for an Old Testament translation with Isidro and Yolanda as translators.

The work struggled along in the early stages, not helped by the distance between the translators and myself, so the United Bible Societies consultant, Bill Mitchell, warned reluctantly of a curtailment. However, the arrival of Juan Toribio, the man overlooked for the New Testament job but a genuine enthusiast for the project, saved the day and brought the work back up to speed.

Juan proved a highly gifted translator and was also a good friend whose sturdy faith and good sense of humour led to a positive approach to life, despite the poverty in which he and his large family lived. Isidro once asked me if translation sessions with him involved plenty of laughter, because Juan was a great man of mirth. They certainly did, not least when we grappled with the Song of Songs! I also recall his amplified translation of the pagan customs at the 'high places' of Canaanite religion; it was so explicit that we could have been accused of producing pornography! We laughed our way through the discussion and the making of the necessary radical changes!

Juan played a further vital role in the Old Testament project: he was responsible for encouraging Ponciano to join the team, a wise, stolid, inscrutable man steeped in his language and culture. He dedicated himself to several of the books, translating by kerosene lamp in his home in the village of Lote 8 after the day's nursing was done. Juan passed away some years back, and as I was finalising this memoir I heard with sadness that Ponciano, too, had gone home to glory.

In ten years we completed the huge task, and so was produced "the first Bible in an authentically Argentine language", to translate the words of SBA President Salvador Dellutri at one of its six launches. This was held in the Teatro Avenida (theatre) in Buenos Aires, following events in Juárez, Santa María, Misión Chaqueña and Salta, and a subsequent one in Córdoba. It was a joy to have Yolanda, Isidro and Juan at that one in the Teatro Avenida in Argentina's capital city.

4
Eureka!

My introduction to the Wichi language came from Bishop Harris and a typescript grammar produced in the 1960s for English speakers. It was helpful as a starter but I learned over the years not to take everything in it as gospel. The way words were spelt could be misleading as to pronunciation, as in the example of *honaj, honat* and *honal* below (Appendix 3), where the sound represented by the *n* turned out to be different in each one. Being with the people and listening carefully helped correct things, together with the insight of language informants such as Francisco.

One thing that puzzled me in that grammar was the lesson devoted to "abstract nouns". It surprised me that a minority language like Wichi should have such abstractions, until one day it dawned that the suffix of such words, *-yaj* or *–hayaj*, was actually equivalent to the English *–ing*, making these nouns gerunds (or verbal nouns) rather than abstractions. So, for example, the word *ohumnhayaj* 'my like, love' is more exactly 'my liking, loving', *–okhajyhayaj* 'my strength' is more accurately 'my being strong', and *owahnhayaj* is 'my permitting, my authorising'. This demonstrates that Wichi is a 'mobile' language which captures life's *activity,* unlike the abstract nouns which so often leave our own languages staid and static.

Are there adjectives in Wichi? Some say yes, I say no! For me the so-called adjectives of that 1960s grammar are really verbs rendering the idea of 'being strong', 'being green' etc. Are there prepositions? Definitely not! One Wichi friend became indignant during a session on Wichi grammar when I said that his language lacked prepositions. I pointed out it didn't need them as Wichi is an agglutinative language – that is, it uses affixes, mainly suffixes, to represent what prepositions convey in our languages. This elasticity can be demonstrated by the root *–mä*, 'sleep', which can be modified by various suffixes subtly to alter its meaning and give the necessary precision:

omähi	I sleep in …
omä'pe	I sleep on …
omäyej	I sleep with …
omäphä	I sleep erect; I close my eyes without sleeping
omählä	I sleep on account of …
omäye	I sleep (somewhere for a purpose)
omäyen	I put to sleep, lay [someone] down …

Another common example is the root *–w'en*, 'see, have' which can be adapted thus:

ow'ene	I see (over there)
ow'enche	I see along; I see going away
ow'enlä	I see coming, approaching
ow'enpe	I see across
ow'enej	I see happen
ow'enho	I have for = I give

and the noun *ow'enek*, vision, something seen

The example early in Part 1 of this memoir is probably the longest word I encountered in Wichi: *olhaihowatshanhit'awethä*, 'we are not feeling sorry for ourselves'. Its components are:

o first person
lhai reflexive
howatshan root = 'feel sorry for'
hit'a negative
wethä plural of continuity

143

One Sunday afternoon in a service in the community of Bazán near Las Lomitas, I heard the pastor pronounce a word in such a way as to make me realise that I'd been confusing two words with distinct though similar meanings, thinking them the same word. The word he used was *lhäy'es*, meaning 'companions'; its singular *lhäy'e* translates the word 'and', indicating the sense of companionship. However, I had confused the plural *lhäy'es* with *lhayes* or *lhayis*, a term indicating pluralisation as in *tewok lhayis*, 'rivers'. This plural could be used with names, so when I was one of two missionaries called Robert we were referred to as *Roberto lhayis*, 'the Robert ones', 'the Roberts'. Quite different, therefore, to *Roberto lhäy'es*, 'Robert's companions'.

It was easy too to confuse similar forms, for example *–ton*, 'pull, drag', and *–tonte*, 'put at a distance', and helpful to realise that the latter, despite sound and appearance, arose out of the common root *tofwe* (or *atofwe)*, meaning 'far, distant'.

These were encouraging eureka moments, except I always wondered how I'd missed them before. Earlier was my discovery that a certain class of verbs as used along the River Pilcomayo lost their distinguishing prefix when a causative suffix was added to alter the meaning from, for example, 'I work' to 'I make [someone or something] work', 'I give [someone] work'. But I won't bore you with this, save to highlight the moral: beware causative suffixes.

5
Your Consultant will see you

The first consultant from the United Bible Societies, Dr Bill Reyburn, is mentioned at the start of Appendix 3. As well as helping us with the orthographical conundrums of Wichi – how best to write the language in light of discoveries since it was first reduced to writing just over a century ago – he was a great raconteur. He recalled how his plans for amending the way the Cree language was written in preparation for a new translation of the Bible were received by an elder. This man stood up in church and announced: "The white man came in the past to take away our lands." *Nodding agreement.* "The white man came to take away our animals." *Nodding agreement.* "The white man came to take away our traditions." *Nodding agreement.* "Now this white man has come to take away our Bibles." *Nodding agreement.*

Tellingly, Bill also reported an episode in an African village when the chief called him and a translation colleague to his house to read to him the first chapters of Mark which they had just completed in the local language. After listening, the chief said, "Have you whites got these writings in your language?" *Yes.* "Have you had them a long time?" *Yes.* "Then why are you whites so bad?"

Goods trains, fog and locksmiths
Our second Consultant was another Bill, Canada-based Scotsman Dr Bill Mitchell, who'd done Bible translation in Peru. He first came in October 1985 at a time of terrible travelling conditions due to early season rain. On my way to meet what I thought was his train I was given a lift to the station through the cloying mud by two gendarmes (frontier policemen) in their jeep. They were also expecting someone on the train, and the story one of them recounted while we waited is reproduced in an appendix to Part 1 of this memoir to show that it's not only expats who suffer from culture shock. I wrote it up the next day while it was still fresh in my mind.

The train arrived at 1am but no Bill. He finally appeared 34 hours later, weary and worn, having come on a goods train. Learning of no transport from Formosa to Juárez because of conditions on the predominantly dirt road which was Highway 81, he'd taken a bus along tarmac right round to Salta, another to Embarcación, stayed at the Mission, been given a lift to the station the previous day at 6am by a missionary, then endured a 17-hour wait before leaving for Juárez. Thankfully it was worth it, his time with Isidro and myself being helpful and encouraging.

Bill visited us once more in the 1980s, and later resumed his consultancy duties when we worked on the Old Testament. His experience as a translator was immensely valuable to us, as was his never-failing encouragement.

Our final consultant was the affable and stimulating Dr Roger Omanson from Louisville, Kentucky. Bearded, balding and bespectacled, with an engagingly warm smile, he first came in October 1988 and his speciality was exegesis and New Testament background, unlike Bill Mitchell's which was in translation for indigenous groups. Roger felt, for example, that Aramaic words such as 'Corban' (Mark 7:11) should be maintained in the translation because the writer deliberately included them for their cultural detail, then translated them for his Greek readers. He also felt we should not insert a phrase in Wichi such as *Tajyäme täja* ('After this', 'Later') in verses such as Mark 3:13 where the original is abrupt, reflecting the writer's style. We didn't, however, follow his advice on these, feeling neither helped Wichi narrative!

On his second visit in 1990 Roger had a journey to rival Bill's first one:

- His American Airlines flight from Miami to Buenos Aires was prevented from landing because of fog. The inexperienced pilot circled for an hour or two and was in danger of running out of fuel, so landed at Montevideo, across the River Plate in Uruguay, with fire engines and ambulances at the ready.

- There was a further delay because American Airlines had no authorisation to use that airport and passengers couldn't get off.

- Negotiations took place to buy fuel, but then the crew had to rest as they'd been working 15 hours.
- Eventually Roger reached Buenos Aires and crossed to the internal airport, but missed the flight to Formosa.
- He flew to Corrientes and crossed the bridge to Resistencia but was now a day late.
- He booked into the Hotel Colón for the night and got up in the morning to leave by bus for Formosa from where he could catch the 10:30 bus to Juárez.
- But his room door had jammed shut and the key wouldn't turn in the lock. A locksmith came but Roger missed his bus to Formosa, eventually arriving there at 11am, too late for the one to Juárez. So he waited the day and caught the overnight one.
- He finally arrived!

Following this unforgettable journey he was able to settle down to some good work with us, as well as producing a few magic tricks to entertain both us and some of the local folk. He advised us to introduce Romans 3 verses 1, 3, 5 and 7 with a phrase such as "Someone might argue" to make the diatribe clear. So we inserted *Elat iche hin'o chik yok ...* in 1 and *Mat elat hin'o äp yok ...* in the others. Roger was a little disturbed that Isidro worried over not producing a translation close in word and structure to the original, as represented by the Reina Valera (RVR). Isidro was doubtless concerned that criticism could be levelled at him by devotees of RVR and literal translation.

A lot of tensions crossed Isidro's mind during those sessions with Roger, including: the camel and the eye of a needle (see Appendix 1); why don't the Rogers of this world have all the answers?; why do translations differ so much?; why can't we be sure that Jesus' brothers were really brothers and not cousins as the Roman Catholics believe?

Got to have a committee
The Reading Committee was a motley group of folk from various parts

147

of the diocese who met from time to time to discuss portions of the translation and controversial issues arising. Always present was Wichi bishop Mario Mariño.

We considered issues of sexuality and our rendering of them and matters such as the use of local trees in the examples in James 3:12 rather than fig-trees, olives and grapes, none of which may be found in the Chaco. The committee liked the idea as it helped contextualise the teaching, but then felt uncomfortable at the idea of an apostle in Palestine writing of Chaco trees and fruits. So we maintained the original ones.

At one of the final meetings during the New Testament project they requested that introductions be made for each book, as in the Spanish Popular Version (DHH). Isidro strangely found this a difficult exercise and most of it was to fall on myself. They also asked that larger numbers be written in both words and numerals: hence *ciento cuarenta y cuatro mil (144,000)* in Revelation 7:4. These numbers had to be in Spanish: the Wichi only have numbers up to two, five or ten, depending on your opinion, and even these can be rather complex. 'Two', for example, is *täkwfwas*, meaning 'a little few'; 'three' is *laj t'unfwaya elh*, 'one without a partner', and 'four' is *t'ufwahtes ihi*, 'partners'. Small wonder the Wichi themselves prefer the Spanish forms today.

Later the committee brought to our notice objections from some readers about an angry Paul's wish for his opponents in Galatians 5:12. So this was changed from the literal 'emasculation' in the New Testament of 1992 to "that they never have children" in the complete Wichi Bible.

6
Translation issues

Many were the challenges we faced with the biblical text, and like all who translate into minority languages we tackled issues such as:

When there is no word

Snow, for example, is not part of the Wichi experience. Where it is used metaphorically we either sought a cultural equivalent as in Proverbs 25:13 (see Appendix 1), or simply used something like "very cold". If non-metaphorically, we usually used a phrase containing the word *fwiy'et* (= cold weather).

Hebrews and many Old Testament books contain several concepts unknown to the Wichi. The Spanish *sacrificio* was used, for example, in the 1962 version, but we preferred to translate by phrases which either included the word *õ'län* (kill), for example, *itshätäy tä õ'länhenpe noch'isukyajay* (Hebrews 9:9 = 'animals put to death for one's sins'), or *t'awayhat* (gift) as in *yachuyaj lhay tä õyen Lhawuk t'awayhata* (subtitle at Leviticus 6:14) = 'the grain that one offers to the Lord'. This helps folk to grasp the meaning.

Sometimes a generic term was used when no specific equivalent was available. In Isaiah 55:13 the lack of pine and myrtle in the Chaco led to the generic "lovely trees".

At the end of Joshua 9:6, for lack of a noun equivalent to 'treaty' we had to use teens of Wichi words to translate 'Make a treaty with us'. The back-translation is: "If you do what we wish, we want you to affirm to us your word so that we stick together and we do not fight against each other". The first six words are a polite way of introducing the request in Wichi. And "affirm a word" was the usual way of capturing the idea of an agreement, covenant or treaty. Incidentally, the 1962 New Testament always rendered this idea by the Spanish word *pacto*. When I asked a class of Wichi students what it meant, no one could answer other than the most intelligent of them – and all he could do was offer a couple of Spanish synonyms from the glossary. This, like in the example of *sacrificio* above, warns of the danger of just using a Spanish term and assuming knowledge and understanding of it.

Making the sense explicit

This was often essential to clarify the meaning. Sometimes, as with the example from Joshua 9:6 above, it meant expanding the verse. In Ezekiel 36:26, "a heart of flesh" was rendered as "inner beings which love me so that you do all my words that I tell you". Earlier in that verse "a heart of stone" was translated as "inner beings which are hard like stones".

2 Corinthians 11:12 is very implicit and the 1962 version is quite unclear. We translated: "But I will continue *not to be a burden to you* [explicit], so that there will be no way for *those so-called apostles that you say are important* to boast that *their work and our work* are not different. *Because they would like us to ask payment from people for the work we do, like them.*"

Culture clashes

Kissing isn't a Wichi habit so phrases for 'suck the cheek' and 'suck the mouth' had been coined. But at the end of some letters such as 2 Corinthians where Paul enjoins the readers to "Greet one another with a holy kiss", we went for an appropriate cultural equivalent: "Greet one another, embrace one another thus making a sign that you are God's children." In Proverbs 24:26, "An honest answer is like a kiss on the lips", Isidro removed the "kiss" metaphor in his draft, replacing it with "others really like what he/she says".

On a similar note, in Ezekiel 25:6 I asked translator Juan for a Wichi equivalent for *habéis ... saltado de alegría* ("you jumped for joy"). He replied, *Ihichet'a* ("There isn't one"), and went on to describe the Wichi as emotionless. For example, he said if a man returned home after three months' working away, there was no greeting of reunion between him and his wife, who carried on her work as normal.

Nevertheless, he added, things are changing as they start to copy the *criollos* – now they shake hands! I witnessed this handshake once as I delivered a young pastor back to his village and his wife after some time apart – though I did notice they also beamed with affection at each other!

Use of direct speech

This is common in Wichi and we used it frequently where indirect speech and other forms are found in Spanish. Mark 1:4 is the classic example, where "John came … preaching a baptism of repentance for the forgiveness of sins" is put into direct speech: "John … spoke to the people and said, 'Change your inner beings and be baptised, so that God will make your sins gone'".

Another instance is Genesis 21:25-26 – "Then Abraham complained to Abimelech about a well of water that Abimelech's servants had seized. But Abimelech said, "I don't know who has done this…."" The Wichi version reads: "Then Abraham spoke to Abimelech and said, 'How is it that your servants have taken a well of water from me?" Abimelech answered and said, "I don't know about that." And the phrase for Abimelech's reply, *Häp tä n'am hanej*, is pure colloquial Wichi.

Metaphors

These can easily be misunderstood and it's rare that the same one translates across languages of peoples far apart culturally. Often we used similes instead, as in Jeremiah 18:20 where, in Wichi, "it is as if they've dug a pit for me" prevents the reader thinking Jeremiah was literally in one. He would be several chapters later! And in Jeremiah 23:1 we needed to avoid a reader thinking that the shepherds mentioned were bucolic workers; so we clarified that they were "the leaders of my people", and then added that their behaviour was *like* shepherds who scatter their sheep and lead them to destruction.

My suggestion of *Wichi Lhäs* (Son of the People) for 'Son of Man' was finally rejected by Isidro and we returned to the established literal

151

Hin'o Lhäs. He quoted examples of *hin'o* being used generally for humanity, and I accepted this.

7
The Dreams and Sayings of Translator Isidro

Dreams

Translation sessions with Isidro were frequently enriched by his recounting of dreams, sometimes with interpretations. Once he dreamed he was wandering among the Wichi, wondering how he could improve their condition, when he came to a beautiful river. But how to get water from it when the land alongside was steep and rock-hard? The only way was to dig down through the stone. Everyone laughed as he began to do this, telling him there was no chance of reaching the water, and he became dispirited. However, he persisted and the water suddenly gushed upwards and came to form another beautiful big river. Meaning? We were translating Romans at the time, a hard, tough task offering little encouragement, but eventually it would bring much blessing.

Another time he dreamed that a certain missionary was suddenly smitten with leprosy which affected his whole body and his 'understanding'. Then God came with a razor blade and cleansed him completely. Isidro interpreted this as the radical effects of sin and God's healing. (I wonder why it was a missionary in the dream?!)

At the same time he dreamed he was preaching to a congregation of headless men, and realised they were without Christ, the Head of the Body. Suddenly the heads came floating along the adjacent river. "Ah", thought Isidro, "now they'll be reunited to Christ." Not so; the heads floated past.

Once he dreamed he was in a service when he spotted what looked like a sheep in the forest. He told the folk it was a puma but they laughed at him. When he got to it he found it was a sheep with a puma's head, reminding him of Paul's warning to the Ephesian Christian leaders in Acts 20:29: "After I leave, savage wolves will come in among you and will not spare the flock." In the dream Isidro attacked it but it escaped. He followed it, failed to catch it, and found the walk back to the village took 1-2 days.

One day he failed to appear for work. He explained it next day by saying he'd had a row with his wife and had gone to the forest to pray. Then at night I appeared to him in a dream and told him (in far better Wichi than I'm capable of) not to let the life that is in him become a corpse.

He dreamed that he and Silverio, a Christian leader from Barrio Obrero in Juárez, were meeting with some nuns about the Wichi alphabet. When he 'proved' that *th* is best suited to the aspirated *t* rather than to the lateral (l) of Richard Hunt's original orthography, the nuns covered their heads and slunk away. Somehow this reminded him of the story of the woman caught in adultery in John 8!

He even dreamed he'd flown with me to the UK and had an interview with Margaret Thatcher. I wonder who came out the stronger!

Sayings

These are some of the man's memorable sayings and tales:

"On the day when the New Testament is launched, there will be banners and flags, but in heaven, not on earth." (Probably due to his reservations about the reception of his work by the Wichi.)

"We don't need to worry about where exactly Jesus was born – we shall see the film one day."

"When we get to heaven we shall meet Paul and ask him what he meant to say in each part of his letters. And if we've got 70% right', we can be satisfied."

"The translation is like drilling for oil [*which was happening to the north near where he grew up*]. The Word has always been there, but only now is it being discovered and brought to the people, and requiring great effort."

154

"Look out for neologisms amongst the Wichi, such as *fwilawos* (tangled up, confused) from the Spanish *fideos* (spaghetti); and *Malvinas* (fighting)." [Malvinas is the Argentine name for the Falklands.]

"Any missionary who defends the 1962 translation against ours should be sent back to England."

"Sometimes I'm like a cyclist instead of a horseman. I use my own strength instead of relying on another's."

"Lord, the work is yours. We are just the pens."

"I was in Carboncito listening to a woman describe how her child had fallen from a tree when a branch broke. She seemed to say he escaped unharmed because *isej ele.* Isej ele?? He was saved by a parrot?? How come?? The woman seemed bright enough. Seemed to know what she was talking about. So I had to accept that somehow a parrot saved the child. Then the woman said *Matche, t'un t'ak,* 'Yes, the strap was strong.' Ah! A dialect problem! Her *ele* (parrot) was really *hele* – her pronunciation of *hilu* (string bag). The strap of the lad's bag had caught on the tree and saved him. Now I understood."

"This passage in John 3 about births reminds me of a lovely custom now lost to the Wichi church. When a child was born in a village, the person leading the service would say at the end, *N'ahoyela n'aelh tä nech'e* (Let's visit the newborn).Then they would go to the house and welcome the child into the world."

"I've discovered the origin of our word *atsinha* 'woman'. Adam woke up to find Eve taken from his rib and exclaimed, *Atsina?* 'What's this?' [A likely story – as likely as his suggestion that Adán (Adam) comes from *Nada* (Spanish for 'nothing') and *Eva* has to do with *ave* (Spanish for 'bird')!!]

"Lord, your work is hard, we're tired and it's easy for us to make mistakes; we're carrying the burden of people needing to benefit from our work." [His prayer after a particularly difficult session on 1 Corinthians 15:1-14.]

"Cuesta mucho limpiar las joyas preciosas" [It's hard work polishing up precious jewels] was part of his prayer after a demanding session on Philippians 2:1-11.

The question of the alleged 'ghost' in Mark 6:49 led Isidro into a long disgression about *ahät lhayis, n'olhahwos, lehusek* (all phenomena of the spirit world) and *hustas*, the little people of the forest seen by many people and whose tracks Isidro insisted he had seen.

His advice to two Chorote translators: "Don't tread on the same thorns that I trod on, following the same tracks."

His advice to a would-be young missionary from Northern Ireland: "Make sure you have your wife behind you and also be better equipped than the early missionaries, because the young people that you'll have to deal with today are better educated and have wider experience."

"An old man, after listening to a sermon on the end of the world (*noj honhat)* remarked on leaving the church: *Olhakli ihihit'a olham. Che noj honhat, ohohiyela olhäse ta ihi Juárez."* (I'm not worried, me. If *noj honhat,* I'll go to my daughter in Juárez.) He understood *noj honhat* in its more 'earthly' sense of 'when the land has gone' or 'when we no longer have land'.

8
Teaching the language

Just as I had been given my introduction to the Wichi language by Bishop Patrick Harris, so I was often asked to teach it to new missionaries and other folk working amongst that people-group. Things started well as my first students, new missionaries Dick and Jen Hines, picked up the language well in Misión Chaqueña where we were all living at the time, and then went on to fluency in Misión La Paz where they lived the next few years. Like me they received great help from Francisco Pérez.

Afterwards, though, my work in this sphere was less successful. Some Anglo-Saxon missionaries were used to communicating with the people in Spanish and both they and the hearers found it strange suddenly to start talking to one another in Wichi. Argentines, meanwhile, found the stark differences in the sound systems of the two languages difficult to overcome; unlike Spanish, Wichi is consonant-based, and its consonantal adaptations, mentioned below, proved too challenging. It was not surprising then that all this, combined with the improving Spanish of the Wichi, especially the younger males, meant that no student progressed very much with the language.

But then a surprise! In 1991 we returned as family to the UK and encountered at a SAMS staff conference a couple who had served as missionaries in Chile and were now preparing to move to Northern Argentina to take on the challenge of helping lead and co-ordinate the Christian Education ministry among the Wichi. I was asked to teach them the language so that when they arrived there they would already have a reasonable grasp of it.

I soon realised that David and Shelley Stokes, British and American respectively, were enthusiastic about their new calling and the learning of a new language and we quickly became friends. "They must be really dedicated", remarked the parish priest of the village church in County Durham where Margaret and I were worshipping at the time during her studies for the ordained ministry. The priest was impressed that David and Shelley drove from Weymouth all the way up to the north-east to study Wichi with me. They made two trips of a fortnight each and I spent two periods with them down in Weymouth. Their commitment overflowed, and I would sometimes hear them going through lessons and vocabulary in the evenings after putting their two young children to bed.

The fruit of this was many years of excellent ministry in the Chaco, only coming to an end in 2021 when David and Shelley retired. So it may be said that my Wichi teaching exploits began and ended well!

9
Other publications

From my very first week of studying Wichi in January 1977, I began to compile a list of words with their Spanish equivalents (where possible), initially on 5"x3" index cards. This grew over the years and once the Bible translation was completed, time was available to turn this into a dictionary. With excellent editorial assistance from missionary Chris Wallis and his Wichi colleague Eduardo Pérez, this was published by the Sociedad Bíblica Argentina in 2016 under the title *Diccionario de la lengua wichí: Wichí-Español*.

Chris and Eduardo were also responsible for the revision of my Wichí grammar, *Wichi Lhämtes: una gramática del idioma wichí con ejercicios*. This work of mine had been published in 1999 by CEPIHA, a branch of the Humanities Faculty of the University of Salta, and ASOCIANA, the social arm of the Anglican Church of Northern Argentina. Originally written in English and translated by former missionary colleague Virginia Patterson, it was designed as a pedagogical grammar to teach the language to non-Wichi speakers. Broadly speaking, lessons were devoted alternately to verbs and nouns and exercises appended to each.

The reordered revision by Chris and Eduardo uses much of the original text but is a systematic description of the Wichi language and an important work of reference. It is based on the dialect spoken in the area of Santa María on the upper River Pilcomayo. I am delighted with the quality and comprehensiveness of this grammar.

One more linguistic publication merits inclusion here. In 2003 the Sociedad Bíblica Argentina and ASOCIANA jointly published *N'atetshan wichi lhämtes*, a course in reading and writing the language based on the alphabet agreed at the seminal gathering of representatives of Wichi from different areas held at Morillo on 30 August 1998 (see Appendix 3). The course was originally taught in August 2000 to 50 Wichi bilingual auxiliary teachers and others from the provinces of Salta, Formosa and Chaco in a conference organised by CEPIHA, ASOCIANA, ENDEPA (Tepeyac Association) and held under the auspices of INAI (National Institute of Indigenous Affairs). Each chapter of the book introduces a letter or digraph (plus the trigraphs *chh* and *tsh)* and includes exercises, reading and comprehension. Its target audience is Wichi speakers who are already able to read and write in Spanish.

Hymn and Service Book

Before these linguistic ventures came the revision and updating of the Wichi Hymn and Service Book. The first meeting of the committee for this took place on 21 September 1989 with representatives from the Pilcomayo, Juárez and Pozo Yacaré. Isidro sang his way through the first half of the existing book, though some of these hymns had unknown and rather dreary, old-fashioned tunes. To bring a bit of modernity to the revision I had translated "Jesus is Lord", "Thine be the glory", "Señor, quién entrará en tu santuario?" (a popular Spanish song based on Psalm 15) and "Thou art worthy". And I sang these translations to the committee. The first met with a deafening silence – "too lively", "no muy wichi" (not very Wichi)! Nevertheless, it made it into the book at number 157.

At the 8th meeting Isidro and Bishop Mario took the decision to omit the second half of the Venite. Mario said that if folk haven't had their *mate* (green tea) beforehand, they fall asleep before it's over! We also included a modern upbeat version translated from English, though the most recent revision has done away with both.

Meeting 23 made me realise how little understood or misunderstood were some of the early Christmas carols. This is due to faulty terminology or grammar, but metaphors and illustrations are also hard for folk to understand. In 'Away in a manger' there was puzzlement over *Lhek yahin lete'pe .... lefwus .... lenhus etc.* 'Come look at his face ... his fingers ... his nose, etc'. Pastor Tránsito also pointed out that a newborn baby doesn't smile, as stanza 2 states. In addition, *Hup ihi näte* seemed incomprehensible (it's meant to mean

160

'the rabbit is in the grass', though it suggests the grass is in the rabbit), and one member misread the last word as *inät* (therefore giving the sense, 'the grass is in the water'). Stanza 3 says, unintentionally, that the animals and bats were not afraid of Jesus instead of *vice versa*.

In meeting 28 Mario pointed out that the first line of the last verse of hymn 82 more naturally refers to selling land *(owom honhat)* than to dying. And in 86 it looks as if the demons are casting out Jesus and the blind healing Jesus. Poetic and grammatical licence are not usually possible in Wichi – you can't put the object first without indicating the subject. For example, *och'isukyaj itäyhat* in 87 implies that sin is forgiving somebody.

We strove hard to remedy these matters and create a new book, which was duly published in 1992. This work has itself been revised in recent years, the latest version being published in 2013.

Appendix 1

Examples from the translation

One of Isidro's favourite Spanish words during translation was *explicitar* – making a text explicit to avoid at best a lack of clear meaning or at worst ambiguity or error. The other translators quickly picked up this requirement. Here are some examples.

Clarifications

Matthew 26:24 = Mark 14:21 = Luke 22:22 Translated fairly literally this verse looked all right. But we realised that "The Son of Man" will go along the way that God's Words in their Container [= Book] say about him" could simply mean in Wichi that Jesus was obedient. Isidro thought that's what the text meant, especially as it could be understood to contrast Jesus' obedience with Judas' disobedience and treachery. We clarified: "The Son of Man will enter suffering and death, just as God's Words in their Container say about him."

Mark 14:30 Did Isidro's rendering of "before the cock crows twice" by *chik ho'o kamaj nachajaho tä y'ip (*when the cock has still not crowed again) necessarily imply 'two times'? He insisted it was clear but Chorote New Testament translator Julián Gómez, who is trilingual and was visiting that day, said it wasn't. We agreed to clarify it and added an introductory sentence to Jesus' words, namely: *"Tonight the cock will crow.* But when it has still not crowed again..." Later on Julián asked me privately if Isidro and I always had arguments!

More words make sense

Romans 9:2-6 is extremely long in Wichi because we needed to make the sense as clear as possible:

(2-4) "There is no time that my thinking hurts *[an idiom meaning 'my thinking always hurts']* as I worry greatly about my others who are my brethren the Israel people, because I see they do not have salvation *[this last clause is a clarificatory addition]*. I say, I wish God would curse me with a curse and bless them with his mercy! I wish he would put *me* far from Christ and put *them* in my place! *[An attempt to clarify the meaning and to avoid what might seem absurd and illogical to the Wichi.]* Because they are those whom God chose in order to make them his children, and he revealed to them himself and his bright greatness. It was they who benefitted from his words that he confirmed to them a long time ago, such as the Law he gave to Moses. And he showed them how they should worship him, and he told them the good things he would give them in the future, and he affirmed these words to them. *[79 words in Wichi from 'Because', as nouns in majority languages often require verb phrases and clauses in Wichi.]*

(5) And their ancestors were Abraham and his descendants *[making 'the patriarchs' explicit]*, and one of their offspring was Christ, the Saviour who is God's Envoy *[= the Messiah]*. May God be praised until it shoots right over there *[an idiom meaning 'for ever']*, he who is chief of all things! Amen.

(6) But when I said, "My others the Israel people do not have salvation *[added to make this verse connect with what has gone before]*, it's as if I'm saying that God's words that he confirmed to their ancestors were not true. But that's not so. Because consider, not all ...."

2 Corinthians 3:1 is another example of making the implicit explicit to convey the true sense: "But when you read this word of mine, perhaps you say, 'Paul and his companions are boasting, as is their custom'. Or you say, 'Paul and his companions should bring letters from other Christians, as other men do, so that we know that they are truly God's servants and we can accept them.' And when we leave you, perhaps you think we should ask of you letters so that other people to whom we take God's word will know that we are truly God's servants and so accept us." This is long, but if the sense is communicated length isn't an issue.

Ephesians 2:11 was translated a little paraphrastically to convey both meaning and mood: "So, come think about the days gone by, you who were not Jews, in whom the sign of cutting one's foreskin was not on your bodies. And the people who make themselves big through that sign that is in their bodies, they call you 'People without the cutting mark.'"

Hebrews 11:8-13 A very challenging portion. The problems were: (a) Who had faith in verse 11 – Sarah or Abraham? (b) Isidro took verse 12 to refer to many descendants born to Abraham while he was still alive (c) Does *pajtha y'inhen*, used by Isidro, indicate that the patriarchs did receive the fulfilment of the promises *once they died*? Probably not, but we amended our text for clarity.

2 Kings 3:20 is another example of a text that had to be amplified for clarification: "And on the next day in the morning, the time came when *the priests in Jerusalem were giving to God a lamb that was killed for the worship of God, just as they do day after day. And it was at that time that the soldiers who were in the desert looked up and saw* water coming from the way that comes from Edom, and it covered the ground."

Jeremiah 48:16 Not all verses come out longer in Wichi! This one is a rare example of the Wichi version being quite a bit shorter than DHH and English versions. DHH has 13 words, NIV 12 – Wichi just 6.

Ezekiel 34:23 and **37:25** "David" was expanded to "One who will be like my servant David", so as not to create the notion of David *redivivus*.

Daniel 7:1 The subtitle was expanded to show that this event happened before that of chapter 5.

Clarifications – where misunderstanding by the translator suggested a problem for the general reader

Matthew 4 verses 7 and **10** I felt it important to check the understanding of the second person in these quotations from Deuteronomy 6. Isidro understood at least the one in verse 7 to be used by Christ as a warning *to Satan* not to tempt God, and I once heard a Wichi preacher take this line using the 1962 version. This is even more perilous in Luke's account where the verse following the command not to tempt God says that Satan left off his tempting of Jesus. I suggested adding a phrase that indicated the command in Deuteronomy (and therefore here too in the Gospels) was for *people* (including Jesus here). Isidro reluctantly accepted this. But subsequent to the publication of the New Testament, and later the complete Bible, he was still questioning the necessity for the addition. I still believe, however, that we have averted a misunderstanding of the text.

Matthew 6 verses 2, 5 and **16** These verses have an identical final sentence. Isidro translated it in three different ways, though all based around the idea that "they have already received their reward", which is the way the 1962 version has it. When I asked him, at verse 2, what he thought their reward was, he said it was their wealth. God had blessed them with riches and so they were able to give alms. It is worth noting that while perfectly understandable, his interpretation goes against verse 1 and is certainly not a necessary inference in 5 and 16. I believe their reward is actually the praise they receive from others.

Isidro was persuaded, admitting that his own 'poverty' and the use of *pajche* in the 1962 version, a word which basically means 'previously', had led him to his own misunderstanding. He suggested we make the implicit explicit, hence our clarification in each verse: "their reward which is that people praise them for what they do".

1 Peter 3:1 Isidro misunderstood the word 'alguno' (DHH) to refer to an unbelieving outsider ('anyone') rather than to an unbelieving husband. In his interpretation the wives' witness of submission would have wider outreach.

Nehemiah 12:12 Isidro translated "heads of priestly families" as "priests with children". However, the focus is not on family life but on authority and headship. We amended to "priests who have authority over their people".

Esther 2:10, 20 Isidro believed the problem for Esther was her having been brought up by her cousin, rather than her (their) Jewishness. So we made this explicit: "But Esther did not say that she was a Jewess, because Mordecai had said to her, 'Do not make known to anyone the people whose daughter you are.'"

Zechariah 11:3 Understandably the roar of the lion was misinterpreted by translator Ponciano as a threat, a roar of ferocity. However, here it's a sound of lament so we put *y'ipwethä tä laj lew'eta*: "roar for loss of their home".

Clarifications – where the Spanish Popular Version (DHH) was prone to mislead

Matthew 10:15 We needed to beware an ambiguity here in DHH which led Isidro to think that the punishment of Sodom and Gomorrah is something from the past rather than for the day of judgment. The verse is comparing the punishment of unreceptive Israelite towns on the future day of judgment with that of Sodom and Gomorrah *on that future day*. We inserted a future verb alongside "Sodom and Gomorrah" to clarify.

Matthew 10:38 It was necessary to use negatives with both main verbs – *nitilhäja* AND *nhänalhin'o*: "He who does not take up his cross and *does not* follow me". Isidro was convinced the saying, as expressed in Spanish (and it's the same in English), refers to one who does follow Jesus but is not prepared to go to the lengths of taking up his cross. The 1962 version could have supported his argument: "He who does not take up his cross when he follows me ..." Much debate ensued before he agreed to insert a second negative.

Hebrews 11:35b Isidro understandably misunderstood this verse in the ambiguous DHH (which relies too heavily on a comma). His version read: "But others died in affliction and did not receive the liberation/salvation in order to enter a better life." However, (a) 'tormento' = torture, not affliction. Isidro interpreted it as spiritual anguish on the part of those without God (b) He overlooked the comma after 'liberados', taking 'resurrection to a new life' to be the result of liberation (c) He understood 'liberation' as spiritual, i.e. salvation.

It took us three months to work through Hebrews, probably the toughest task we had. But the longest was Matthew, a tale of six months.

Translate by a Wichi phrase or term rather than use a difficult Spanish term

The 1962 version kept many Spanish terms, such as *circuncisión, sacrificio, pacto* (covenant) and *ofrenda* (offering). Translators Isidro and Juan were minded to go along with these, but such terms are not universally understood by the Wichi, can appear obstructive or

167

meaningless to the reader, and cause him or her to miss the point of what is actually 'happening' as represented by them. See Chapter 6 (above) for examples of this.

However, in Mark 5:9 = Luke 8:30 where the 1962 version left the name of the demoniac as the Spanish 'Legión', Isidro wanted to maintain this. However, I thought it better to look for a Wichi word that brought out something of the sense, rather as theologian Tom Wright has done with his use of 'Regiment' in his recent translation of the New Testament. The word which seemed to offer itself was *Nifwotas,* meaning both an epidemic and a band of warriors. Isidro was never very convinced, however, probably because he'd always seen the man as simply called "Legion" - that was, for Isidro, simply his name. In the end a kind of compromise was reached by giving the man the name "Wujpey", meaning "Many". Nevertheless, this was disappointing because it fails to capture the battle going on in the man.

On a lighter note...

Matthew 20:10 = Mark 14:6 somehow got through our first draft with the possible meaning, "Leave the woman alone, let her do what she does to me because she's very beautiful"! Thanks to one of our consultants, this brought us notoriety in the form of inclusion on the final page of an issue of *The Bible Translator* journal, a page always devoted in those days to translation bloopers.

Luke 1:79 Isidro defended his literal translation of 'the shadow of death' *(n'ot'ilek lehupel)* by saying that although it's not an expression he's ever heard among the people, "they must learn it because it's a nice phrase". It's in the final version, and also in Isaiah 9:2.

Luke 9:10b After we'd avoided translating as "to Bethsaida", because Jesus and the disciples didn't actually get there, Isidro said, "The translators of the Spanish Popular Version should follow our translation, not we theirs!" We put: "And Jesus took them aside and

168

said, 'Let's go to the town of Bethsaida'".

John 2:6 Our first draft gave the impression that the Jews had to wash themselves *in* the jars! This too merited a mention on the infamous last page of *The Bible Translator*.

Romans 13:1-7 Isidro felt this passage could be misunderstood if translated as it stands. So: "Can we add to 'you must submit to the authorities' the phrase 'when they say/do what is right'"? No! But living in Argentina at the time you could understand his concern.

Philippians 4:15 We followed the interpretation of DHH which concludes: "you sent me offerings of thanksgiving (in exchange) for the spiritual help you had received". Isidro suggested using *tä lethatayhlä* for 'in exchange for', but then decided a careless reader might read it as *letatayhlä* – thus understanding it as 'you opposed the spiritual help you had received'! An alternative to *lethatayhlä* was found in the verb *lew'enay n'oho'pe* to convey the idea of exchange.

Colossians 3:16 Isidro saved the day when we were doing the final read-through of this verse by pointing out that our *Is chik lechoyejwethä akäjyaj* for "Sing with joy" from the verb root *–choy* 'sing' could equally be read as "Wipe your bottoms with joy" from the verb root *-cho*. Blushingly we rephrased.

2 Thessalonians 3:14 He noted that our original *yej lhen ama*, used (wrongly, as it turned out) for "do not associate with", could also mean 'do not catch mice'. Paul surely had better things on his mind than the salvation, or destruction, of rodents.

1 Timothy 2:12 To "I do not permit a woman to teach …" Isidro wanted to add *ayej* 'for the time being' – that is, until they gained experience. We didn't.

Deuteronomy 32:10 Isidro did not know the Spanish metaphor "la niña de sus ojos" (the apple of his eye"; literally 'the little girl of his eyes'). But his ostensibly inaccurate translation, "like a man cares for his daughter", is perfectly acceptable and appropriate here!

Joshua 10:11 A bit of liberal theology in Isidro's draft! Unable to believe in hailstones killing people, he changed to 'rocks from the mountains'. We reverted to hailstones!

1 Kings 4:33 Translator Juan provided an 'ecological version' of this verse: "Solomon did not like trees to be misused .... Nor did he think it right to kill fish for no good reason, nor animals, birds or creatures that crawl." Why? I have no idea, other than he might have interpreted RVR's "Salomón disertó sobre" as referring to Solomon giving a lecture – and therefore suggested what opinions the king might have proffered! Typically the affable Juan laughed his way through our discussion!

Nehemiah 3:3 The Fish Gate was translated as "the gate that fishermen pass through". The literal *W'ahat Pe* also means 'fish fat' and would more naturally be understood by the Wichi in that way! The same is true of Sheep Gate in verse 1.

Job 28:18a Translator Ponciano was unfamiliar with 'coral' – except the coral-snake! So his draft version of DHH ("Wisdom is more precious than coral") was "Wisdom exceeds a coral-snake". Perhaps it's more lethal!

Psalm 69:17 Our translation of the first line was originally the literal *Chumlä akawona*, but this was modified to *Chum n'ohlä tä ohäpe akawo* as the first version looks dangerously like *Chumlä akawon'a*, "Take your hat"!

Making a monkey of other versions (all in a good spirit)

Matthew 13:25 We used the Spanish *cizaña* (RVR) because of its similarity to wheat. Isidro insisted you can't sow 'mala hierba' (DHH text); such weeds just grow by themselves.

Matthew 18:32 We suggested that the translation of the last phrase in DHH, Good News Bible (GNB) and New International Version (NIV) is incorrect. The debtor did not ask to be forgiven his debt (verse 26). Isidro pointed out this error when I read him a back-translation of GNB. We simply put "When you pleaded with me".

Ephesians 4:17 Beware the 1962 Wichi version which misinterprets 'vanity' (RV) as pride rather than futility. We put *letichunhayajay tä najit lahaya,* "worthless thinking".

Genesis 31:31 Jacob's answer in this verse is to the question in verse 27, not that of verse 30. We inserted "The reason that I didn't tell you I was leaving was that I was afraid ..." No version consulted at the time clarified this, though New Living Translation (NLT) and Contemporary English Version (CEV) have since done so.

Camels and compromises

Matthew 19:24 Comparatives can pose problems in Wichi, and when there's also a grammatical feature such as the hyperbole in this verse, the problems increase. The normal way of expressing a comparative (other than the use of the verb *inu'pe* 'exceed') is to state two opposites. So "it's colder today than yesterday" = *Chayokwe naji, techäjche ifwalana* 'Warm yesterday, cold today'. Isidro translated Matthew 19:24 similarly to the 1962 version: "It is not difficult for a camel to pass through the eye of a needle. But it is difficult for a rich man to enter the kingdom of heaven."

The first sentence seemed to me absurd and I wanted to put: "It is

171

difficult for a camel to pass through the eye of a needle. But it is very very difficult for a rich man to enter the kingdom of heaven." Isidro refused to accept this, arguing that the 1962 version was perfectly understood by the Wichi as highlighting the difficulty for the rich to enter the kingdom. And he said Mr Grubb, its translator, had preached on this text to illustrate the improbable ease with which a repentant sinner can enter the kingdom. Perhaps he did, but he can't have believed that's what Jesus' words here meant.

Yet "miracles are possible", said Isidro, "and even camels can get through needles" (??). He had a bee in his bonnet, or a needle in his eye, about it all and it proved such a divisive issue than when raised in a session with Translations Consultant Roger Omanson, who supported my argument, Isidro's emotions overcame his reason as he asked how God could allow such a 'mistake' in a translation. In the end, however, we translated in the sense of 1962 but added an emphatic *Yachajo tä oyok, ¡matche tä atha!* (I repeat; it's very difficult!) at the end. An example of compromise, I fear.

And on the subject of compromise....

Romans 8:28 "Also we know that people who love God, we whom God calls according to his will, everything that is with us helps us so that we benefit." For me this wasn't the best interpretation. I'd have preferred to have God or the Holy Spirit as the subject, making things work together for good, rather than our "everything". However, Isidro preferred the above interpretation, it follows the 1962 version's understanding, it's comprehensive – and under these circumstances to structure the verse to fit the other interpretations was extremely difficult.

Out of order

John 12:12-19 While drafting his translation of this section, Isidro found the order of events in his Spanish versions confusing. (The same applies in English versions.) So to help the Wichi reader he put the verses in this order: 12, 14, 17, 18, 13, 15, 16, 19. After careful study I accepted this reordering, as did Translations Consultant Bill Mitchell who was impressed enough to recommend it be written up as a short article for *The Bible Translator* journal. It appeared in an issue during the 1980s.

Genesis 47:4 The Wichi don't come so quickly to their requests and plans as did the Israelites! So we placed the sentence about the famine in Canaan and lack of pasture first as the reason for Jacob's family coming to Egypt, before their wish and request to stay.

Nehemiah 8:3-5 Isidro noted an apparent discrepancy. In verse 3 Ezra reads the Law, while in verse 5 he opens the book (of the Law to read it). So Isidro changed the order to 4, 5, 3. I accepted this, though it's equally possible that verse 3 acts as a summary of what is to follow.

Features and figures of speech

John 6:61 "¿Hä lelätay olhämettso?" is Isidro's translation of "Does this offend you?", where the root *lät* (feel) has the extended sense of 'be offended'. He used an example of a church leader's nephew's reaction to his uncle's non-acceptance of him as a church council member even though he'd been voted on by other folk: *Olät owithok lhämet* ("I feel my uncle's words" = I'm offended by them).

2 Corinthians Irony and sarcasm in this letter, especially in chapters 10-13, are difficult to convey in a language that uses them little.

Exodus 21:24-25 These "eye for an eye" verses are a good example of how noun phrases often have to be translated by clauses, and of how to deal with the lack of prepositions in Wichi (their meaning is conveyed by suffixes). The Wichi version reads: "Or if he damages another's eye, his eye should also be damaged" etc.

1 Kings 22:13 "Te ruego que" (DHH) is too polite. Juan ignored it and translated in suitably direct Wichi, *Huwa ämlhi,* "Come on, speak..."

Psalm 103:11 To translate literally, comparing God's love with the distance of sky from earth, suggested to Isidro that it's unattainable. Better a demetaphorised, if rather colourless, version: *Matche tä lajit lepesa lehumnhayaj,* "His love is truly endless".

Psalm 147:3 'Brokenhearted' is not natural in Wichi and 'wounds' can mislead.   Isidro's draft was an excellent piece of functional equivalence: "He heals people whose sadness exists, and puts away what hurts their thinking."

Jeremiah 31:36-37 and **33:20-26** In these passages the negative hyperbole of the Spanish versions was made positive, such as "I will never leave my people … I will never abandon them."

Cultural equivalents

Revelation 3:20 In his draft Isidro avoided the idea of knocking on a door, which is not a Wichi custom. Instead he had Jesus drawing the attention of the person inside by calling out to him/her, something more culturally appropriate and also leading well into the following "the one who hears my voice".

Proverbs 25:13 Isidro produced an appropriate cultural equivalent here rather than use the metaphor of 'snow': "A good messenger … is like something cold that a man drinks on a hot day". A version to savour in the sub-tropical Chaco!

Jeremiah 22:8-9 The oddity of "the LORD" on the lips of pagans is a problem because in Wichi his title and name are *Lhawuk*, "Our Master". In these verses (and in many like them throughout the Old

Testament) it was changed to *lewuk* or *lewuk dios*, "their master" or "their master God".

Luke 12:55 With the north wind bringing the hot weather in Argentina, we faced three possible solutions to this problem verse: (a) Leave it as it is and let preachers and teachers explain (b) Change 'south wind' to 'north wind' or 'hot' to 'cold' (c) Leave it as it is and add a footnote. The 1962 version chose (b) but today's better educated Wichi would realise this made Jesus strangely ignorant of his country's weather. We chose (c) with a brief explanatory footnote: "Where the people of Israel live, the south wind is the hot wind", which is just seven words in Wichi.

What does it mean?

Matthew 5:32 Following a suggestion from Roger Omanson based on recent scholarly opinion, and bearing in mind the note in the DHH Biblia de Estudio, we adopted 'incest' as our interpretation of the kind of sexual immorality referred to by Jesus. (Though in a Reading Committee meeting one pastor got the idea incest was being commended rather than condemned!) Nevertheless, I think our interpretation may need to be reviewed in future.

Appendix 2

Matthew 5:3-12: the Beatitudes

This dialogue, based on our work on the passage, was presented as a 'WICHI BIBLE STUDY' to the General Council of the South American Mission Society in November 2002, shortly after publication of the Wichi Bible. It has also been presented to other church groups and conferences as an insight into the challenge facing translator and exegete in seeking to render a difficult passage into an indigenous language. My words are in ordinary type, Isidro's in italic.

Isidro, you start your draft of these beatitudes with "One's good blessing". Why "blessing" and not "happiness" as in the Spanish Popular Version (DHH)?

Because it's more than just happiness. It's something God gives, creates, for a person.

Agreed. Then how about indicating that this blessing comes from God – God's good blessing, rather than "One's good blessing" as you have?

Yes, agreed.

Now, tell me. Why do we need to say 'good blessing'? Aren't all blessings good? Look at the Spanish word – it has the sense of 'goodness' in the first syllable.

Roberto, let me explain. The word –käpfwayaj which we use for 'blessing' can be good or bad. I know that today most people think of it as good because of its use in the 1962 New Testament and in the Wichi liturgy. But strictly speaking it's a neutral term. In your language maybe it's just good. In the white man's language [Spanish] it's just good. But in our Wichi, it's either.

Yolanda, who's on the Translation Reading Committee, told me one

176

day she'd been puzzled by your addition of 'good'. She said, "My thinking said, 'What is the reason that Isidro adds 'good'...?' Then one day I visited my mother in the pueblo and heard her use the word *-käpfwayaj* for 'curse'". So it can have either sense. You're right – we should, therefore, make it clear.

Just as I said.

But therefore...what does this word mean exactly? I mean, a word by itself which can mean either blessing or curse – that's what I don't understand.

Ah, the missionaries... they come from their lovely homes far away ... they don't understand our words. Some of them, like you, almost, almost...

What have lovely homes got to do with it? Anyway I'm asking you so I will know.

Come pay attention to my words. The word käpfwaye means "create", "call into existence". So we can say "God käpfwayed so that the earth existed". And in our people's myths the old rogue Thokfwaj [Little Uncle] would käpfway himself so as to turn or create himself into an animal, a bird, a woman, etc. And the devil might käpfway somebody with something bad. So it's the right word for blessing, provided we put 'good' alongside it, because when God blesses somebody, he creates for them something they hadn't got already. Might be material. Might be feeling – blessing somebody with peace. That's what blessing is – giving them something which will do them good.

Yes, I understand.

And one other thing. Remember Jesus feeding the 5000? Ikäpfwaye, blessed, so that the bread and fish became enough for everybody. It was Jesus's creation.

Excellent. Thank you for explaining that to me. But now we've got another major problem in verse 3: "Blessed are the poor in spirit".

Is it the Holy Spirit?

I don't think so. But if we translate "poor in their spirits/inner beings" literally – "whose inner beings are poor" – somebody once

177

referred it to "non-Christians" – people whose spiritual lives are poor.
Yes, it can mean that.

I'm going to suggest a wordy translation. We'll be accused of doing a paraphrase, I expect, by the Pentecostals.
They think the whole lot's a paraphrase, don't they?

Yes, they have a different view of translation. If it's not literal word-for-word, it's paraphrase. Anyway, here's my suggestion for "Blessed are the poor in spirit": "God's good blessing is with those who know that it is only God's kindness that they benefit from, and they continuously want it."
Good. But permit me, in my humble condition and with very poor theological knowledge, to suggest a slight adjustment at the end. Instead of "and they continuously want it", it's better Wichi to put it into their mouths, and write: "and they say, 'That's what I need'."

Right, agreed. Though I can't see what that's got to do with theology. Anyway, are you happy that that sentence accurately communicates what Jesus meant by "the poor in spirit"? [I repeat sentence]
Yes. And that should be all of us, right?

Now how about "for theirs is the Kingdom of Heaven"? For Kingdom we use "chiefdom", right? There aren't too many Wichi kings about! Hey, Isidro, do you ever feel like being a king? Isidro, king of the Wichi?
Oh, me, no. I'm an insignificant man. Sometimes the devil tempts me to carry myself along [= be proud]. But really I'm a... nothing, nobody, a man of no consequence. But... if the people wanted me to be, say ... a bishop, maybe I'd have to consider it.

I wish I hadn't raised that. Must stick to the task. Er... I notice you've put "possessors of his chiefdom" for "theirs is the Kingdom of Heaven". How about "children" rather than "possessors"?
No, "possessors" is better. God gives them the Kingdom.

So you're happy the Wichi will grasp the sense of what Jesus is saying.
Yes.

I should tell you that when somebody in England saw our possible draft, they thought it really brought out the sense.

Perhaps they'll use our version as a guide for future translations in English and Spanish.

I doubt it! Chorote, maybe. Er... I think we need to be humble. We mustn't "carry ourselves along". Hey, we've spent so long over one verse. I don't think the rest will occupy us so much.

v.4. God's good blessing is with those whose being sad exists. God will make them happy. No word for mourn?

No.

Not many words for emotions, are there? *-lhakli, -fwitajayaj, -käjyaj*, cover many words in Spanish and English.

They're sufficient for what we need to feel.

v.5 God's good blessing is with those who make themselves ones who are nothings. That's the same expression you used a minute ago talking about yourself. A nothing. Now you're using it to translate "meek". And no one word for "inherit", so what have we got?

They shall receive the land that God promises them.

v.6 God's good blessing is with those who are hungry and thirsty to want what God wishes.

Roberto, we have a problem here. In Wichi we can talk about being hungry for food and other things - such as, er, women. But we can only be thirsty for drink.

So what do we do then?

We'll have to put something like "those who it is as if they are thirsty to want what God wishes." Because they're not really thirsty. It's a strong desire.

So a simile to replace a metaphor?

If you say so.

Hey, that word you've got for "God will fill them" is a long one. Yipsaynhiyejena!

Yes, we've got some long words in Wichi.

v.7 God's good blessing is with those who are kind to others. Again, there's one word that covers kindness, compassion, mercy etc. But it's a key word in Wichi, isn't it?

If you say so.

Well, I mean, it comes from the root for 'poor'. And to show kindness etc. literally means 'consider as poor'. P'elitsaj…p'altsen… Wichi so often say, op'elitsaj - I'm poor. And they often come to the door and say "is chik lep'altsenn'o" – literally "Please treat me as poor" – in other words "be kind to me", "do me some act of kindness", "give me something". Rightly or wrongly, it's fundamental to the way the Wichi think. "We're poor", "Consider us as poor". It implies a need for help (originally from within the community, but now increasingly from those outside it). Help us!! So this verse is really saying: "God's good blessing is with those who regard others as poor (and who therefore automatically help them). God will regard them as poor (and will therefore automatically help them).

(With a smile) If you say so, Roberto.

No, but I mean <u>we</u> have much to learn from you people. Caring for one another. Seeing others as in need of our help.

Roberto, the other day I had to visit Pastor X's house. His wife was preparing a meal. In the old days they'd have shared it with me. But they didn't. They waited until I'd finished my conversation and left, and then they ate. Years ago they'd have 'regarded me as poor', in need, a member of their community with a need, and they'd have shared their food with me. But the community spirit is dying – at least, in these communities in the towns. In the villages, by the river, folk still 'regard each other as poor' and look after each other. Yes, our language does teach us things about ourselves. But while the language lives on, some of the values it represents are slowly disappearing. Bishop Mario says we spend too much time aping the white people and their values. And while I don't always agree with Mario ... I think he's right in this.

PAUSE FOR THOUGHT

v.8 God's good blessing is with those whose inner beings are alone. "Inner beings", not "hearts".

No, my heart, ot'otle, is just something beating in my body. Nothing else. As a Wichi I am made of ot'isan, ohusek and olhämet [body, inner being and speech].

Ah, that's why speech is so important. And God's speech. This book we're creating.

Or God's creating through us. Because I'm just a pen in God's hand as I translate. Or a man carrying precious jewels across a desert.

And what about "whose inner beings are <u>alone</u>". Alone = pure.

Right. Because there's nothing with them. Nothing false attached to them, no pride or self-centredness or greed or anything added on. That's what 'pure' means in my language. That's why the word for 'alone' is also the word for 'pure'.

v.9 God's good blessing is with those who make others' peace. I like that. Those who create peace for others.

That's a fundamental role for a pastor, but of course for any Christian.

And "They shall be called children of God" = "He will say, Those are my children."

I like that.

And of course otamsek, the word for peace, is what all Wichi seek and long for. It's like a Hebrew idea – shalom. Wellbeing, quiet, peace, absence of problems, time to be.

No fighting, no trouble, no worry. I and my family have what we need.

v.10-12 I'll just read them, because I think your translation is excellent. "God's good blessing is with those to whom people put their fighting when they do what he wishes. They are indeed the possessors of his chiefdom. God's good blessing is with you when people mock you because you follow me and put to you their fighting and their diverse slanderings. Do your joy, make yourselves happy, because big will be your reward in the sky. Because so it was with the prophets a long time ago in the past, people put to them their fighting."

Yes, the prophets a long time ago in the past. And also the first Wichi evangelists. They had aggression and slander put against them from the witchdoctors and others when they first took the gospel to folk. But big is their reward in the sky. And come think about how God has blessed their work here. Think of what he's CREATED – ikäpfwaye – his church amongst us who are Wichi, I mean, we who are God's children.

Roberto, shall we pray a while?

Appendix 3
Sounds and Letters

Over the years we were blessed with visits from Regional Translation Consultants from the United Bible Societies, starting in mid-1981 with Dr Bill Reyburn, an American with experience of linguistic work. He helped with the challenges of the Wichi orthography, the way in which the language was written. This had been developed by pioneer missionary Richard Hunt, an exceptionally gifted linguist, in the second decade of the twentieth century, and provided the basis for a subsequent adaptation by ourselves in light of developing linguistic research and understanding through the century.

Hunt's orthography came under scrutiny because it did not approximate to Spanish and voices were raised to adapt it in that direction. However, while Wichi and Spanish have some sounds in common, there are many differences: Wichi is consonant-based, Spanish is vowel-based; Wichi has a rich adaptation of, for example, plosive sounds, so there are three 't' sounds, three 'p' sounds, and no less than six 'k/q' sounds. The distinctions are in aspiration, non-aspiration and glottalisation. In the case of the 't' plosive, we now write the non-aspirated sound as *t*, the aspirated as *th*, and the glottalised sound as *t'*. Glottalisation was not usually written by Hunt, but now it is generally represented by an apostrophe, thus allowing the spelling to differentiate between, for example, *ochen* 'I send' and *och'en* 'I stretch', and between *yikne* 'he went away (I saw him go)' and *yikn'e* 'he went away (so I'm told)'.

Voicelessness occurs with some nasal sounds, and is represented with a following *h* – *mh, nh*. So it is now possible to make clear differentiation between, for example, *honaj* 'afternoon, evening', *honhat* 'land, earth', and *hon'al* 'weeds'. These were previously written as *honaj, honat, honal*.

One nasalised sound, the voiceless palatal semivowel, had been written in a number of ways in the old orthography: y, ñ, iñ are but three. We chose *yh*. Part of the logic for this is that, for example, the plural noun suffix *-hay*, when it follows a root ending in *y*, creates the voiceless palatal semivowel sound. So the plural of *m'ay-ek* [root *m'ay* + singular suffix *–ek*] 'thing' is *m'ay-hay* [root *m'ay* + plural suffix *–hay*] 'things', with the voiceless palatal semivowel sound being created in pronunciation by the root ending *y* and the following suffix initial aspirate. Writing this sound as *yh* has therefore a certain appropriateness.

Down the years the most debated part of the orthography had been the use of *th* to represent a lateral fricative. Hunt was noting a similarity (though not an identity) between this sound and the common English *th*, but this representation was neither accurate (the Wichi sound is undoubtedly a lateral [*l* sound]) nor diplomatic as its frequency, especially at the beginning of words, made the language look English and led to accusations of missionary colonialism. So what to do? Reyburn suggested *hl* and this looked promising. However, the sequence of aspirate (*h* sound) followed by lateral (*l*) occurs in a few common words such as *nehläs* 'hunger; famine'. So we decided to reverse it to *lh* and were guided, amongst other things, by the phenomenon of the sequence of a morpheme ending in *l* and one beginning with an aspirate creating the fricative *lh* sound. For example, the final *l* of *hin'ol* 'men' followed by the initial aspirate of the diminutive suffix *–has* creates the lateral fricative sound, which is now appropriately written as *lh* – *hin'olhas* (literally 'little men' but used of young boys).

The vowel panorama was cleared up with six identified and represented: *a, e, i, o, u, ä*. This last was sometimes written *ö* in the old orthography, but more often than not confused with *a* or *o*.

The Wichi language does not have a passive voice; however, it uses an impersonal third person singular form of the verb to convey the passive sense. The prefixes to indicate this, depending on the dialect area, are *õ-* or *õ'-* (the verb root dictates which) and *n'o-*. For example, the verb *oton*, I pull, has the forms *õ'ton* or *n'oton* to translate the

184

passive idea 'is pulled' (literally 'one pulls').

The writing of the impersonal third person form by the prefix *õ-* or *õ'-* is important, as in the earlier orthography it was simply represented by *o-*, thus confusing it with the first person prefix: hence, with our previous example the form *oton* was used for both 'I pull' and 'is pulled'. This led to ambiguity, as in the 1962 translation of Mark 10:40 where Jesus tells his disciples James and John that "to sit at my right or left is not for me to grant. These places belong to those for whom they have been prepared." The 1962 version has Jesus correctly saying that he cannot give those places to them, but then seemingly has him giving them to those for whom they are prepared. The confusion lies in the fact that the obvious way of reading the second sentence in Wichi is, "I will give them to those for whom they are prepared" (*o*) whereas the translator was really intending the passive sense, "they will be given": literally "one will give them", represented nowadays by the impersonal prefix *õ*. But as this form *õ* was not written in 1962, a muddled meaning was being communicated. Just for the record, the 2002 version avoids the passive sense altogether by indicating God as the preparer of those places.

All these and other modifications were worked through with Isidro and other thoughtful Wichi, and it was gratifying to find young people enthusing over them. The feeling is that greater accuracy in representation gives the language greater dignity. The first meeting of the Reading Committee in 1982 focused on the orthography and I was pleasantly surprised to find them in favour of almost all the changes suggested by Isidro and myself. The saga of the orthography is always unfinished business, but in 1998 at a meeting in the town of Morillo, agreement was reached after lengthy discussion by Wichi delegates from most parts of the Chaco on how each sound should be represented, and the 'Morillo Alphabet' has now been adopted as the official Wichi orthography. The document created on that date, 30 August 1998, requested: (1) the acceptance of this orthography in place of any other (2) that it be recognised at all levels of Argentine society (3) that it be taught in schools and Wichi-speaking

185

communities (4) that teachers and bilingual auxiliaries be trained to use it in schools where there are Wichi children.

A year earlier two *criolla* teachers helping the Wichi children to read and write in their own language in the school in Barrio Obrero asked me to write a paper on the orthography to counter a professor of linguistics in Formosa who insisted the orthography should be approximated to Spanish. Not long afterwards they told me he'd backed down – though not necessarily as a result of my paper! Nevertheless, I imagine that approximation to the forms of the national language will always have its supporters.

The subtle differences between sounds sometimes got me into trouble with Isidro over a mispronunciation. One day reading back to him our translation of the Christmas story in Luke 2, I had the shepherds looking after their little knives instead of their sheep – *tson'atas* = sheep, *tsonhathas* = little knives. And the sign for the shepherds, on my error-strewn tongue that day, was a baby coming towards them rather than just a baby – *lew'enla* = you will see, *lew'enlä* = you see approaching.

Bible launch in Juárez: translators Ponciano, Juan and Isidro with author

Launch in Buenos Aires: Isidro, Bishop David, Yolanda and Juan

Chris Wallis in his office

Häp Pablo laka carta
tä ichene Dios leles tä ihi

FILIPOS

Pablo ilesayen laka cartana tä ihi n'op'onthi. Yäme tä lakäjyaj ihi t'at, wet ihumnhen
t'at Dios leles tä ihi Filipos. Ifwenho lhamel nilhokej m'ak tä iyej tä ihi n'op'onthi,
yämhiyet'ak lelhakli ihi, mat yäme tä takhajay t'at, wet matche tä lhayen Cristo lakawoya,
wet tek nowaye t'ilek. Wet yok, "Olham ow'atshancheyaj häpe t'at Cristo, wet chik oy'il,
häp tä lhäy'e lhip tä oisej" (1.12 yäk 21).

Inityenej wichi tä ihi Filipos tä is chik lhaikhajyenhen, wet ichaye Lhawuk, wet iwoye
t'at m'ak tä Dios lhämet ne'tek iwoye, wet hin'älit lehusey tä tek lhaichäjwethä, hätet iwoye
Cristo tä tek lhaichäjlhi (1.27 yäk 2.18).

Pablo ichene len'okhayaj häp Dios leles

1 [1] Amtena ipuhfwas tä lheyayhi hupuy tä Filipos,[a] häp amel tä ahäpehen Dios leles tä lep'akayej Cristo Jesús. Olham Pablo lhäy'e Timoteo, Jesucristo lakawos n'ohen, ochene olhämetna nilhokej amel, lhäy'e aka líderes, lhäy'e lech'otfwas.

Filipos

[2] Is chik Dios Lhajcha lhäy'e Lhawuk Jesucristo iti amejen lep'altsenyaj lhäy'e atamsek.

Pablo iwo t'alhyaja'pe Dios leles

[3] Tä otichunpej amchehen, owo graciasayej oka Dios, [4] wet tä owopej ot'alhyaja'pe nilhokej amel, wuj tä okäjyaj ihi. [5] Tsi y'alhaip'ajtejwek Dios

Silätyaj tä Is, tälhe ifwalahte nech'e oi'amejen yäk nämena. [6] Wet ohanej tä kalelhäj tä Dios, häp lham tä iwo tesa lechumet tä is tä i'amejen, tujlhahichela pajla'tha wak'alh, chik nichäte ifwala chik Cristo Jesús tapil alhoho. [7] Is alhoho otichunhayajay tä mälhyejentso, tsi wuj tä ohumin nilhokej amel. Tä oihi n'op'onthi, wok ifwalas tä olhaikhajyenpe Dios Silätyaj tä Is tä oyäme tä matche t'at, amel alep'ajtitay n'oyej tä Dios iti n'amejen lep'altsenyaj. [8] Wet Dios ihanej tä lhäy'e lhip tä otipej amejen ohumnhayaj tä tälho Cristo Jesús lehumnhayaj.

[9] Oy'alhyen amehen Dios yämthilek lhäy'epej lhip lhäy'epej lhip ahumnhayaj, häpkhilek matche tä lehanej tä lhäm kalelhäj m'ak at chik häpe, [10] wet letshupyenepej m'ak tä is. Wet chik mälhhiyejatso m'ak chik lewoyaye, häpkhilek ts'ilak ahusey wet tek ihichela m'ak chik Cristo ayen tesayej chik tapil alhoho. [11] Mat Jesucristo tach'otla amehen yämthilek lewoyaye m'ayhay tä wuj tä isen, häpkhilek ö'wujyen wet ö'wunit häp Dios.

[a] 1.1 Ap.Lh 16.12

Page of Wichi Bible

We give God the glory for all that has been achieved, and continues to be achieved, in the lives of the Wichi people and their beloved Anglican Church in the 111 years since Richard Hunt and his fellow pioneers arrived in the Chaco in 1911. *N'awunit Lhawuk! Let us praise our Lord!*